Leadership Resilience

For Peter Gilbert.

Leadership is one of four main areas of work on which Peter has focused in his professional life. Now we are all holding him in our thoughts as he battles with the debilitating effects of Motor Neurone Disease.

Leadership
Resilience

Lessons for Leaders from the Policing Frontline

Edited by

JONATHAN SMITH and
GINGER CHARLES

GOWER

Gower Applied Business Research
Our programme provides leaders, practitioners, scholars and researchers with thought provoking, cutting edge books that combine conceptual insights, interdisciplinary rigour and practical relevance in key areas of business and management.

Published by
Gower Publishing Limited
Wey Court East
Union Road
Farnham
Surrey, GU9 7PT
England

Ashgate Publishing Company
110 Cherry Street
Suite 3-1
Burlington, VT 05401-3818
USA

www.gowerpublishing.com

British Library Cataloguing in Publication Data
A catalogue record for this book is available from the British Library.

The Library of Congress has cataloged the printed edition as follows:
Smith, Jonathan Ashley.
    Leadership resilience : lessons for leaders from the policing frontline / by Jonathan Smith and Ginger Charles.
        pages cm
    Includes bibliographical references and index.
    ISBN 978-1-4094-4068-0 (hardback : alk. paper) – ISBN 978-1-4094-4069-7 (ebook) – ISBN 978-1-4094-7470-8 (epub)
    1. Police. 2. Leadership. 3. Police – community relations. 4. Police – Job stress. I. Charles, Ginger. II. Title.

    HV7921.S62 2013
    363.2068'4–dc23
                                                                    2013011906
ISBN 9781409440680 (hbk)
ISBN 9781409440697 (ebk – PDF)
ISBN 9781409474708 (ebk – ePUB)

Printed in the United Kingdom by Henry Ling Limited, at the Dorset Press, Dorchester, DT1 1HD

Contents

List of Figures and Table

Figures

Table

About the Editors

Dr Ginger Charles

Ginger Charles has worked as a police officer in the United States since 1986. She is currently a police sergeant, leading up to 25 detectives in the Criminal Investigations Bureau (Persons Crimes) at Arvada Police Department in Colorado. Ginger received her PhD in Health Psychology from Saybrook Graduate School and Research Center in 2005. Having worked in the police community for 25 years, she has recognized and experienced the trauma and hardships police officers and leaders encounter daily in their profession.

Most of Ginger's police career has been within the patrol function. This has provided a unique experience of "living in the petri dish" of her research as she has shared the experience of trauma, crises, and destruction in the police community. It has become her clear intention to conduct research identifying solutions to help police officers survive and thrive in their careers and beyond, while maintaining their mental, emotional, physical, and spiritual health.

Currently, Ginger's research is focused on health risk factors in the law enforcement community. In addition, she has explored how spirituality affects police officers' work as well as their health.

Dr Jonathan Smith

Jonathan Smith is a Senior Lecturer at the Lord Ashcroft International Business School at Anglia Ruskin University in Cambridge in the UK, where he has led a number of leadership and human resource management (HRM) programmes. He designs and facilitates innovative masters-level courses in leadership, strategy, organizational change, and HRM. Jonathan also coaches and supports leaders and human resources professionals in the research, design and implementation of best practice initiatives in organizations. His current research, consulting, and development interests are focused on organizational, team, and individual transformation through spiritual leadership; development and training within the police, and sustainable development for businesses.

Jonathan has experience in a variety of managerial and training roles, in a number of public and private sector organizations. Prior to working at the university, he was a Director of Studies at the UK's National Police Training and Development Authority, working to shape the training agenda to achieve world-class performance within police training. His PhD explored the relevance of spirituality within police training. He also has an MA in Human Resource Management and a first class honours degree in Mechanical Engineering. He is the co-author with John Rayment of a leadership book recently published by Gower entitled *MisLeadership: Prevalence, Causes and Consequences* (2011), and the author or co-author of numerous journal articles, including "The Relevance of Spirituality in Policing: A Dual Analysis", *International Journal of Police Science and Management* (2012); "Spirituality, Leadership and Values in the NHS", *International Journal of Leadership in Public Services* (2010); "Globally Fit Leadership: Four Steps Forward", *Journal of Global Responsibility* (2010), and "Breaking the Silence: The Traumatic Circle of Policing", *International Journal of Police Science and Management* (2008).

About the Contributors

Sir Peter Fahy

Sir Peter Fahy is Chief Constable of Greater Manchester Police (GMP), the United Kingdom's third largest police force.

He grew up in East London and joined the police in 1981, and is currently the Association of Chief Police Officers (ACPO) lead of Specials Constabulary, ACPO lead on workforce development issues, and Director of the Strategic Leadership Course at the National Police Leadership College Bramshill. Before taking up this post at GMP in 2008, he was the Chief Constable with Cheshire Constabulary, a post he had held since 2002. Prior to that he was Assistant Chief Constable at Surrey, and held positions with the Hertfordshire and West Midlands forces.

Sir Peter has had wide experience of policing inner city and rural areas, and has held a number of command positions. He has experience of leading murder investigations and major complaint inquiries. Throughout his career as a chief officer he has been a strong advocate of police reform and innovation.

Sir Peter holds the Queen's Police Medal (QPM), awarded to police officers in the United Kingdom and Commonwealth for gallantry or distinguished service, and was knighted in the 2012 Birthday Honours for services to policing.

Eric Kellogg

Sergeant Eric Kellogg was in the military for ten years prior to becoming a police officer. During his service, he earned his BS in Criminal Justice from the University of Nebraska-Lincoln. Prior to becoming a police officer, he worked as a youth and family counsellor in both Lincoln, Nebraska and Grand Rapids,

Michigan. In 1994 he joined the Grand Rapids, Michigan Police Department, where he worked as a Patrol Officer, a tactical team member and a detective.

In 2005, Eric accepted a position as police officer with the City of Arvada. He worked in a variety of patrol positions prior to his promotion to Sergeant in 2010. He has been married for 23 years and has two children.

Wendy Kipple

Sergeant Wendy Kipple has worked in law enforcement for 21 years, beginning her career at the Summit County Sheriff's Office in 1989 as a Corrections Deputy. In 1993 she was hired by the Dillon Police Department, and in 2000 was promoted to Sergeant. She is also a certified Crime Scene Investigator, Fingerprint Examiner and Evidence Custodian. Wendy was a Canine Handler for 13 years, as well as riding as a Mounted Patrol Officer during the summers at the Dillon Police Department. Wendy is a member and current Vice President of the Rocky Mountain Division for the International Association for Identification, and is past President of the Colorado Association for Property and Evidence Technicians.

Wendy is also the Chief Deputy Coroner for the Summit County Coroner's Office, where she has worked for twenty years and served under four different coroners. Wendy also recently obtained her Board Fellow certification with the American Board of Medicolegal Death Investigators – a certification that is difficult to obtain, and she is one of only three people in Colorado to have achieved that level of certification in the death investigation field.

Wendy is a member of the federal disaster response team DMORT (Disaster Mortuary Operational Response Team), as a Medicolegal Death Investigator. Wendy responded with the DMORT Team to Louisiana in the wake of Hurricane Katrina and spent a total of nine weeks deployed there to assist in recovery and identification of the deceased as a result of the hurricane, as well as re-identifying the numerous displaced caskets as a result of Hurricanes Katrina and Rita.

Wendy lives in Fairplay, Colorado with her husband and daughter, and in her spare time enjoys her horses, reading, hiking, camping, and doing custom leather work as a creative outlet.

Andrew A. Malcolm

During an extensive career in the UK Police Service, Andrew Malcolm worked in various operational roles, including the Criminal Investigation Department and a specialist unit dealing with public disorder and searches of major crime scenes. He policed during many incidents of major public disorder and was a Public Order Instructor responsible for training officers in riot control techniques and strategy. He ended his career as an Operational Inspector after a period engaged in Leadership and Management Development of newly promoted police officers. On leaving the police, he worked in both the public and private sectors, including a period within the NHS, again in leadership development, before answering a call to ordained ministry in the Church of England. Andrew obtained an MSc in Security Management from Leicester University and a BA in Theology as well as an MRes degree from Manchester Metropolitan University, where his work focused on areas of faith and spirituality in the workplace. He continues this research, combining it with his role as a parish priest.

Tim Meaklim

Tim Meaklim worked as a police officer in Northern Ireland and England for thirty years. He has a PhD in Education and has worked in a range of senior positions within learning and development. Since leaving the police service, Tim has worked as an independent management and learning consultant and a development coach. He has a wide range of experience in leadership, research and education within the UK and internationally. He has a particular interest in ensuring that learning is transferred to the workplace and makes an impact on organizational effectiveness.

Ronald J. Walsh Jr

Born and raised in Long Island, New York, Ronald Walsh is currently a Deputy Inspector with the Nassau County Police Department. He began his law enforcement career with the US Department of Justice as a Special Agent with the then Immigration and Naturalization Service in New York City (NYC). In 1989, Ronald joined the NYC Police Department, graduating from the Police Academy as Class Valedictorian. After three years as a Patrol Officer, he accepted an opportunity to join the Nassau County Police Department on Long Island, again graduating as Valedictorian.

During his tenure with Nassau, Ronald has held the positions of Patrol Officer, Plain Clothes Officer, Problem Oriented Police Officer, Crime Analyst, Sergeant, Lieutenant and Detective Lieutenant, Captain, Deputy Inspector and has also been Commanding Officer or Deputy Commanding Officer of the following units: Community Affairs, Community Safety Unit, Public Safety Section, Property Bureau, Uniform Section, the Police Operations Section, Second Precinct, and Tactical Field Services (consisting of the Bureau of Special Operations, Canine Unit, Mounted Unit, Emergency Services Unit and Homeland Security). In 2008, Ronald graduated from the FBI National Academy in Quantico, Virginia, and most recently earned his MA in Public Administration from Marist College, Poughkeepsie, NY.

Ronald served nine years as an elected member of the Locust Valley Central School District, Board of Education. A former Life Time Drug Free World Champion Power Lifter, he also teaches in the School of Education at Hofstra University on Long Island and has been invited to lecture on Spirituality in Law Enforcement, at the British Association for the Study of Spirituality's International Conference in Windsor, UK.

Reviews of *Leadership Resilience*

Leadership with integrity and effectiveness has always been a major challenge, and never more so than in the global crises we face today. Leaders need resilience, and editors Jonathan Smith and Ginger Charles are in a prime position to enlighten us on its importance and how to build it. With a focus on the police service, who are so often walking the boundaries of society, the authors provide us with vivid narratives and practical ways of moving forward to meet challenges with purpose and inner strength, through experience and reflective practice. I welcome the holistic approach, bringing mind, body and spirit together to lead people into the future.

Peter Gilbert, Emeritus Professor, Staffordshire University, UK

Such a rich collection of powerful case studies on resilience amongst the police. Immediately, by using the reflections and questions, I could see the learning and application to Principals in FE Colleges. The editors' approach to understanding spirituality in the workplace is clear, insightful and opens the territory more widely. A refreshing, practical and thoughtful contribution to leadership in the public sector.

Lynne Sedgmore CBE, Executive Director of the 157 Group of FE Colleges

A compelling book, bringing together the personal and very affecting accounts written by police officers, with analysis of these accounts. The analysis – like the best literary criticism – helps us return to the police narratives with new eyes, and learn even more from them. The police service, like most professions, can be dominated by accounts of efficiency and effectiveness. Yet real police officers can be driven by personal motivations, a sense of purpose or duty, a commitment to care. Resilience is indispensable, as the police face life and death experiences, and social pressures – from colleagues and from the public – tempting *them to a combative or cynical approach to their work. Smith and Charles show how the police account for their lives and careers, and thereby provide lessons for all professionals in dealing with their responsibilities.*

Julian Stern, York St John University, UK

Ever wonder how those in policing do what they do, or what we might learn from them? We so often call upon them to go behind the societal veneer and deal with problems most of us choose to close our eyes to. We don't want to know about it, we just want them to fix it. How do police officers and the police community build the resilience to deal with these difficult problems, and what is the personal cost to the officers that serve our communities? Ginger Charles and Jonathan Smith address deep-rooted issues faced by the law enforcement community and the role spirituality plays behind the thin blue line. Is this just a job or is it a calling? You may be surprised by the answers you will get from this book. The authors dare to create their own path, researching the ways policing deals with the enormous challenges they face, and drawing lessons from this about developing resilience that are applicable to a wide range of leadership roles. They unabashedly look at the role spirituality plays in policing, leadership and resilience, and the lives of law enforcement officers. This will make you look at policing, leadership, those that do it, and resilience and spirituality in a unique and fresh way. It's a book that will stretch your mind and make you think.

Link Strate, Commander, Criminal Investigations,
Arvada Police Department

Introduction

1

We have written this book in an effort to assist leaders with the challenging role they perform. Leaders in the vast majority of cases do an amazing job. All too often they are unrecognized and undervalued even though they are the lifeblood of our families, our organizations, our communities and our society.

Leadership in all its guises is a demanding and challenging role to take on, and with globalization, increasing complexity, the rapid pace of change, and increasing expectations across the world it is only becoming more so. Whilst leadership capability and knowledge about how to perform the role effectively has no doubt increased considerably, this has by no means matched the large growth in demand and expectation placed upon leaders today, particularly in this time of financial and planetary crisis, upheaval and funding cutbacks that are being experienced in many parts of the world, where more is being expected with less. As a result, the gap between leadership capability and demands is becoming ever wider. This is one of the reasons why Rayment and Smith (2011) argue that we are currently experiencing a leadership crisis globally. We must also recognize that the leaders performing these enormous roles are not superhuman; they are just human beings, with all their frailties, worries and imperfections. This places huge pressures upon leaders, and as we shall detail later in this Introduction, this is having many negative impacts on leaders in terms of stress, poor physical and mental health, and burnout.

So how do leaders cope with the challenges they face today? How do they remain fit and strong, and prosper and thrive in such an environment of challenge, complexity, and change? How do leaders cope with the toxic work environment that is all too often seen and which can be worsened with redundancies, closures, financial cuts and all the people issues associated with these? What training and support do they have to enable them to cope effectively? In our experience, leaders are often provided with very little support, guidance or training in these areas, and are often left to just muddle through the best they can. In their own desperate searches for ways to cope, some leaders fall, become isolated, and are drawn to unhealthy coping strategies, seeking solace in many things, including sex, alcohol and drugs, as crutches just to help them survive the day.

The authors have been privileged to work and be able to conduct research within the police environment, both in US and in the UK. Police officers regularly deal with sometimes unimaginable and very challenging situations. Here they are often operating at the margins – between life and death, good and evil, health and illness, love and hate, success and failure, legal and illegal, right and wrong. These situations raise some of the most fundamental and important questions any person has to face, and at some point in all our lives we are all likely to be wrestling with at least some of these types of questions. Police officers experience many extraordinary situations, and deal with these using extraordinary skills and strategies, and yet these police officers, too, are just human beings – they do not employ superpowers to cope, nor are they immune from imperfections.

The police organization is well developed in terms of training and support mechanisms that are in place to support officers in the challenging role they perform, but this is often unseen and also under-valued. The central tenet of this book is our argument that police officers themselves and the police organization as a whole have developed some quite extraordinary ways of dealing with the demands they face. They have developed huge amounts of resilience, and also effective ways of building this resilience. Often this is not recognized in police organizations or agencies, nor in society in general. Of course, the situation within the police organization is not perfect, and there is still a long way to go. The challenges police officers face on a regular basis still have some major negative impacts on both the policing community and wider society in terms of police officer suicides, ill health, relationship breakdowns, and the use of ineffective coping mechanisms such as recourse to drugs and alcohol. Despite the enormous challenges clearly evident in undertaking the policing role and some of the negative impacts, however, the authors have discovered from their research that the vast majority of police officers are:

> *extremely resilient and demonstrate high levels of self-control, compassion, professionalism and love for the work they have chosen to do. Their dedication to service is for many inspiring, revealing some of the noblest acts of self-sacrifice and altruism. These officers appear to have an ability to transform negative experiences, redirect their emotionally*

*charged frustrations and move from feelings of victimisation to using
the experience to create new meaning and compassion.*
(Smith and Charles 2010: 321)

We are interested in these success stories, the positive examples of high levels of resilience being demonstrated every day. Our focus in this book is not just on helping police officers, though. It focuses on leadership more generally, at all levels, in all countries, and in all organizations, including the emergency services and police. From extensive research, personal leadership experience, and teaching, the authors have come to realize that many of the challenges faced by leaders in general are similar to the challenges experienced by police officers. Isolation experienced by people in leadership roles – particularly senior positions – unable to show personal emotions, coping with very demanding roles, working effectively with people who are confused, frustrated, angry, and delivering bad news such as redundancies and severe financial cutbacks are just some examples of the current leadership challenges which police officers have wide experience and training in dealing with. Within the policing environment, however, the authors argue that these challenges are more pronounced and exaggerated, and therefore easier to identify than they may be the case in other leadership positions.

So how do these resilient police officers do it, how do they cope? How do they deal with the extraordinary situations they see on a regular basis? And can leaders generally learn from this about how they might build their own and others' resilience to enable them and the organizations they work within to cope more effectively in the challenging, changing, and complex environments in which they operate?

Our Approach

This book is not a traditional text on resilience, stress, or leadership. It does not contain large amounts of theoretical ideas, facts, and figures on resilience, leadership, or how leaders cope. It is a book about practice, practical application, and example. We use police officers' own narratives extensively to draw real-life practical examples of how ordinary people cope – with extraordinary events, and also with the dilemmas and difficulties which they experience in doing this. This will provide leaders with direct examples of how officers have become resilient through the experience. We then seek to draw lessons from these experiences, both for the wide variety of people undertaking some form of leadership role as well as for the police community specifically. Most importantly, the book also raises questions for you, the reader, to reflect on and answer for yourself, as well as offering you encouragement to raise further questions and keep the dialogue going.

In this book we argue that leaders in all organizations and at all levels can learn something from how the police organization as well as individual officers cope with the challenging nature of the role they perform. From this we hope leaders can build greater levels of resilience for themselves, and for their organizations, so they and the people they lead are better equipped to cope with the ever-increasing demands that are placed upon them. Resilience is key, not just for leaders' own health and wellbeing, but also for the organizations they lead and the societies they are a part of. As Loehr and Schwartz highlight: "Leaders are the stewards of organisational energy [resilience] ... they inspire or demoralise others, first by how effectively they manage their own energy and next by how well they manage, focus, invest and renew the collective energy of those they lead" (Loehr and Schwartz 2003: 5).

This book raises a lot of questions, many quite deep and challenging. You can choose to simply skim over these questions and read the book for general points about leadership and resilience, but the book also offers you the opportunity to embark on a more significant personal journey of building your own and others' resilience. This journey can take place at whatever stage you are at in your life, as you can always become more resilient.

If you wish to embark on this more significant journey, we would ask you to pause for a moment and identify how you are going to find the time and energy to do this so that you will be able to reflect effectively on the questions raised in the book. It will not be easy, particularly if you are feeling that your resilience is quite low anyway – which is quite likely since you are reading this book and possibly wanting to travel on this journey. The first thing that may be useful is to develop a clear picture as to why you want to read this book: What will be better for you when you have done this? What will the new, more resilient you look like? What will it feel like? What can you see yourself doing? What will you be able to achieve that you do not feel able to now? Is there a person you know who you seek to be more like in the way they cope with the challenges they encounter? What is it specifically that they do that you want to try to emulate? Be as specific as you can with your answers to these questions.

When you have reflected on these points, it may be useful to develop a plan of how you are going to work through the book. Be kind to yourself, focus, and take a small step at a time, perhaps reflecting on one question each day, and reward yourself in some way when you have achieved this. Bear in mind that you may be reflecting on some difficult questions at some point in your journey. What support do you have to assist you with these? You may wish to draw on family and friends to help you, as talking through the issues and questions that are raised can certainly help. Also consider any support mechanisms you may have in your work environment, such as human resources or counselling departments that you could talk through difficult questions with. Not that this entire book is going to be difficult – we hope the vast majority will be enjoyable, engaging, interesting, rewarding, and exciting.

Before we embark on the main body of the book, the police officers' narratives, it will be useful to introduce some of the terms we are exploring. In the following four sections we will introduce resilience, stress, fitness, and spirituality, beginning with resilience.

Resilience

According to the *Merriam-Webster Dictionary*, resilience is the "ability to recover from or adjust easily to misfortune or change". It is not the same as strength, with which resilience is often confused. Strength enables you to resist or remain unaffected in the face of life's difficulties and challenges. As the above definition highlights, resilient individuals are moved by misfortunes or change, they are not robots, they do feel sadness, fear, and pain, but they are able to recover easily from this. Ideally, they can also "adjust" to this "misfortune or change" and move to an even more resilient state. Resilience, then, is that ineffable quality that seems to distinguish those who face challenges and fail from those who are knocked down by life yet come back stronger than ever. Rather than letting failure overcome them and drain their resolve, resilient people somehow find a way to carry on and grow stronger from the experience.

We argue, as does the Chartered Institute of Personnel and Development (CIPD) in the UK (2011b), that in the increasingly and endlessly turbulent context of today's working world, the resilience of both individuals and organizations is paramount in order to survive and thrive.

The resilience we talk about here is different from, though in many ways connected to, an interpretation of resilience commonly seen within the emergency services environment, such as the UK's National Resilience Programme.[1] This programme aims to strengthen national and local resilience by improving the infrastructure, and capability of the Fire and Rescue Services so they can respond more effectively to natural disasters, large-scale accidents, the threat of terrorism, as well as day-to-day incidents. Our focus in this book is not on these structural policies and procedures as much as the people aspects of resilience in organizations, including the Fire and Rescue Services.

CAN RESILIENCE BE DEVELOPED?

This is a key question to begin our exploration with, because if resilience cannot be developed there is little point in leaders studying the area or reading this book – or for that matter, in our writing it! To allay any concerns you have here, we believe firmly that resilience can be developed – many thousands of police officers are testament to this. A number of research studies and training activities also suggest clearly that resilience is something that can be developed (see, for example, Alexander et al. 2012). Brigadier General Cornum (2012), who until recently led the $125 million emotional fitness regime for the US military, has also shown that resilience can be developed through her work with the US Army since 2008. Of course, there are some elements of resilience that are undoubtedly part of individuals' make-up and cannot be changed, but we argue that many aspects of a person's attitude, approach, and behaviour related to resilience can be developed and improved.

We also believe that a powerful way for leaders to develop their own and others' resilience is by exploring and reflecting for themselves upon examples of how others cope. Whilst the situations discussed are unlikely to be exactly the same, as Cornum (2012) identifies, with resilience we are talking about transferable skills that can be applied in many different situations – hence the narrative approach we have adopted in this book.

Our emphasis here is on building the skills and resources that are necessary for greater resilience, and being as proactive as we can in building these skills prior to difficulties arising. It seems of much less benefit to sit back and leave it until people experience problems in coping, and then invest large amounts of money in treating or counselling these people, and on training others to identify those who are having problems coping with the stressful nature of their jobs.

---

1   https://fireresilience.cfoa.org.uk.

There are many very effective and successful programmes in the police and military that seek to identify and help people when they have problems, and we do not wish to devalue these, but we argue that in many ways it is too late to leave it until people experience problems.

Building resilience is a major personal and organizational issue, and it needs to be managed effectively and proactively.

GlaxoSmithKline, one of the leading pharmaceutical companies internationally, is an example of an organization that is proactive in this area, and is doing a great deal of work to develop resilience in its leaders and employees. It applies the following definition of resilience in its work on enhancing the effectiveness of individual employees and teams. We find this useful in encapsulating what this book seeks to assist you to do:

> *[Resilience is] the ability to be successful, personally and professionally, in a highly pressured, fast-paced and continuously changing environment.*
>
> *(Campbell in Casey and Corday 2007)*

A HOLISTIC APPROACH

There has been a great deal of work and research into resilience, and one major aspect of this focuses on developing emotional resilience. As an example, Business in the Community has developed a useful *Emotional Resilience Toolkit* (Business in the Community 2008) which provides practical guidance on promoting the resilience of individuals and teams in organizations as part of an integrated health and wellbeing programme. In this, it uses a definition of emotional resilience by Vielife (as cited in Business in the Community 2008: 10), who suggests that emotional resilience is: "the attitude and skill set of an individual allowing them to cope with great efficiency and effectiveness in periods of change and stress".

We agree that one of the keys to building resilience, as emphasized in this definition, is the "attitude and skill set of an individual". However, we argue that the attitude and skill set required does not just relate to emotions, and there are important elements beyond both emotions and the individual that have to be considered. Kevin Gilmartin, a clinical psychologist who specializes in issues in law enforcement, has produced an excellent book, *Emotional Survival for Law Enforcement: A Guide for Officers and their Families* (Gilmartin 2002), which identifies some important aspects with respect to building emotional resilience. Again, though, he only focuses on the emotional aspects to resilience.

Beddoes-Jones (2012: 46) goes further than just emotional resilience, and highlights physical, mental, and emotional resilience, but does not explore how these different aspects can be developed. We still argue that there is a vital component missing, and as we shall go on to explore later in this Introduction, we argue that resilience needs to be considered as a much broader and more holistic concept which includes physical, mental, emotional, and spiritual components.

To end this brief introduction to resilience, we draw on Peterson et al. (2008), who suggest that resilient individuals are:

> *characterised by a staunch view of reality. They are very logical in their interpretations of setbacks – what is in their control, out of their control, and options for taking action … this brain activity leads to the development of "realistic" optimism as well as the motivational processes involved for pursuing the courses of action related to confidence and the strategies devised for overcoming life's obstacles.*

In many ways, we feel this is an excellent description of the vast majority of police officers.

Stress

A great deal of research has also been undertaken in relation to stress and its causes, people's reactions, consequences, and management. It is not the purpose of this text to replicate this. Our interest here is in understanding a little about stress, linking it to resilience, and looking at how leaders can develop greater resilience to cope with the stress that comes from the significant challenges they experience in their leadership roles. We are interested in this because, as Green and Humphrey (2012: 34) show, stress can greatly undermine resilience.

Stress is now regularly identified as a major difficulty in organizations across the world, and the ability to cope effectively with this stress connects us to our resilience focus. According to the CIPD (2011a), stress is the most common cause of long-term sickness absence in the UK. This stress at work seems to be increasing as a result of the economic downturn, with a third of employers reporting an increase in stress-related absence over the last year, with the situation particularly marked in the public sector (CIPD 2011a). Workers blame workloads and management styles, according to the survey. The survey also revealed that the median cost of absence across all sectors was £600 per employee per year, rising to £889 in the public sector. According to the Health and Safety Executive (HSE 2010), an estimated 9.8 million working days were lost in the UK through work-related stress. Every person experiencing work-related stress was absent from work for an estimated 22.6 days. MIND, a leading charity for mental health, estimates that the cost of mental health problems in England alone is £32 billion, and suggests that by 2020 depression and stress will be second only to chronic heart disease as an international health burden (in terms of cause of death, disability, incapacity to work, and the toll on medical services).

Stress is not just a factor in the UK, though, and in a global survey of 1,000 corporations across 15 countries Esmond (2012) identified that stress was a significant issue in the workplace, and her research found that over the last two years it had become more so. This survey found that approximately 60 per cent of workers in significant global economies experienced increased workplace stress. China had the highest rise in workplace stress (86 per cent), while workers in larger companies worldwide (over 1,000 workers and more) were nearly twice as likely to suffer from stress.

Research by the International Stress Management Association (ISMA) found that 53 per cent of workers had experienced stress at work during the past 12 months. A quarter said they needed time off work as a result. Too much work is the most common cause of stress, with almost three-quarters citing it as the reason. Stressors include deadline pressures (62 per cent), unsupportive work environment (40 per cent), and problems with maintaining an acceptable work–life balance (40 per cent). More than half said that stress was damaging their health, 65 per cent believed it was reducing job satisfaction, and 41 per cent felt it was lowering productivity. ISMA Chairman Carole Spiers argues: "If we were talking about a flu epidemic rather than stress at work there would be a public outcry about the scale of the problem. But while given sufficient time flu tends to go away of its own accord, stress at work certainly does not" (cited in *Personnel Today* 2001).

Stress is also a major factor within the police, other emergency services and the military. Bayliss et al. (2010: 2) identify policing as one of the most stressful of all occupations. Alexander et al. (2012) note that around 40 per cent of police officers report stress, with the three most significant aspects of stressful work being "under pressure to get results", "having to meet deadlines" and "having to attend to paperwork". Smith and Charles (2010: 321) summarize some of the implications, resulting issues, and costs from stress in operational policing: for example, 400 officer suicides per year; average age of death for a law enforcement officer 10–15 years earlier than the rest of the population; divorce rate for police officers twice that of non-law enforcement officers; the rate of substance abuse in the police culture double that of the rest of society; high levels of absence, long-term sickness, domestic violence, and drug and alcohol abuse for police officers. These are all testaments to the hugely demanding and costly nature of policing.

What all this clearly points to is that stress is a major factor in organizations across the world, and has major implications for leaders, either directly on themselves, indirectly through the staff they lead, or for the organizations they work in. There is an important and urgent need to explore how to assist people to cope with the challenges and stresses they experience on a daily basis. This applies to the police as well as contemporary organizations more generally. Exploring ways to help leaders to develop greater resilience seems a key element in this, and if this book can help just a few to develop effective ways of coping with this stress and in some small way reduce the financial and psychological burden on leaders, then it will have done its job.

Professor Richard Lazarus, an authority on stress for over forty years, suggests that stress is a: "condition or feeling experienced when a person perceives that demands exceed the personal and social resources the individual is able to mobilize" (Lazarus 1966).

If Lazarus and his quotation above are correct, then one aspect of resilience seems to be connected to developing the "personal and social resources that a person is able to mobilize" in order to cope with particular demands. This quotation also highlights that resilience is not just focused on individuals' resources, as we discussed earlier in the section on "Resilience", but includes the need for a broader consideration and holistic approach.

Seyle argues that stress is not necessarily something bad. He says:

> *Stress is not necessarily undesirable. It all depends on how you take it. The stress of failure, humiliation, or infection is detrimental; but that of exhilarating, creative, successful work is beneficial ....*

Stress cannot and should not be avoided. Everybody is always under some degree of stress. Even while quietly asleep our heart must continue to beat, our lungs to breathe, and even our brain works in the form of dreams. Stress can be avoided only by dying. The statement "He is under stress" [sic] is just as meaningless as "He is running a temperature." What we actually refer to by means of such phrases is an excess of stress or of body temperature.

(Seyle 1956)

Seyle coined the term "eustress" – a positive stress resulting from exhilarating, creative, and successful work. This can be beneficial, and can motivate and energize people. Seyle (1956) also argues that the biochemical effects of stress are experienced irrespective of whether the situation is positive or negative and it is how the person reacts to the situation that shows whether the stress is positive or negative. As William Shakespeare suggests in *Hamlet* (Act II, Scene II): "There is nothing either good or bad but thinking makes it so."

This is a key point to pause and reflect on for a moment. Can you think of stressful experiences you have had that you interpreted in a negative way? Could they have been interpreted in a more positive way? If so, what would it have taken to change the way you interpreted these situations?

Taking Seyle's ideas, it seems that developing resilience may have two components for you to consider:

1.   learning to interpret the biochemical effects of stress that you experience in your body in a positive rather than negative way;

2.   developing the personal and social resources that you are able to mobilize in order to deal with the demands placed upon you.

Some aspects of these resources that you are able to mobilize lie within you. However, we argue that this is not the only resource that is available, and there are many areas that transcend yourself that you can draw on and that can be beneficial. This identifies social resources, in terms of people and organizations. It can be extremely beneficial to talk to others and draw on the expertise of outside specialist organizations for support.

Figure 1.1 shows a way you can identify the social resources and support mechanisms you draw on. This can help raise your awareness of what and who you draw on for support, which areas you need to develop further, and which areas you perhaps over-rely on. One of the difficulties for leaders is that their commitment to the job, and the constant and ever-increasing demands that are placed upon them, can mean that their lives become more and more associated with their jobs. Their identity can become all wrapped up in the roles they perform at work. This can have implications for the leaders' range of support mechanisms, in that they shrink as the leaders become increasingly associated with the jobs they perform.

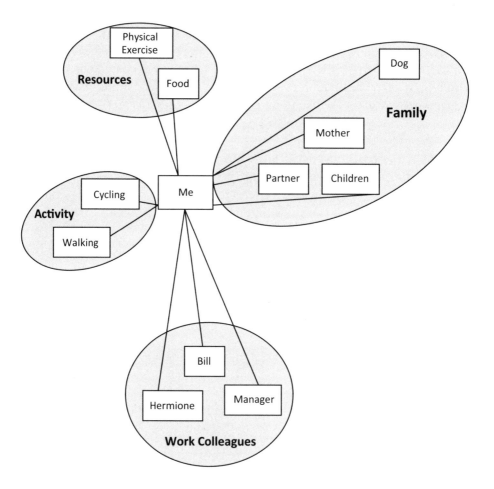

Figure 1.1   Support mechanism mapping

You may find it useful to complete one of these mapping exercises for your own situation. If so, begin by identifying all the different people, activities, and resources that you draw on for support. Cluster these into different categories to assist your exploration. As you identify these, make the distance of the item from the centre represent how important and close this aspect or person is to you. The closer to the centre it is, the more significant it is in your life. Figure 1.1 shows the start of this mapping process.

We invite you to produce one of these maps for yourself now.

When you have done this, stand back a little and have a look at what it is saying. What are your most significant support mechanisms? Is the balance right for you? Has the range of support mechanisms you draw upon enlarged or reduced over time? Why is this? Do you need to develop more, or bring some aspects closer to you? Are there things that you need to become less reliant on?

Nixon (1976) argues that stress can have positive or negative effects on performance, and this depends on the level of stress experienced. He proposes an inverted U-shaped curve to represent this, as we have illustrated in Figure 1.2, to show the positive and negative effects that stress can have on performance.

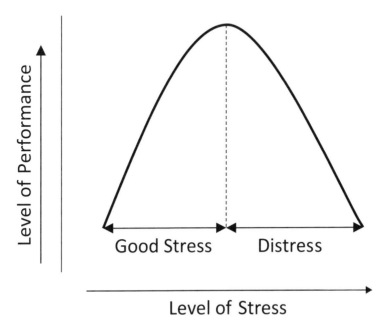

Figure 1.2   The positive and negative impacts of stress

It seems that in seeking to develop greater resilience, what we are really trying to do is flatten the peak of this reaction to stress and move it to the right a little, as illustrated in Figure 1.3.

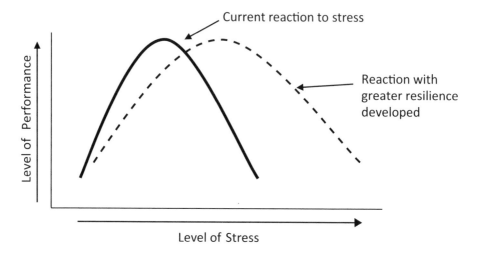

Figure 1.3   Illustration of the impact of resilience on the stress curve

If you drew a graph of your performance as stress increased, what would this look like? How might you flatten the peak and move it to the right, as we have illustrated in Figure 1.3?

An important aspect of resilience that we are particularly interested in is relation to the spiritual resources that are available to us. Both Scott (2011) and Cornum (2012) also identify this spiritual dimension as an important aspect of resilience. Are there aspects you would label as spiritual in the support mapping you have completed?

We are all likely at some point in our lives to experience things which are very difficult and challenging. We may experience something so powerful that the "normal" coping strategies and support mechanism we employ on a daily basis are simply not sufficient, and even the most resilient people can find themselves in difficulties. It is possible that the spiritual dimension, which we could already be drawing on regularly, is particularly important, and may be our greatest source of strength and resilience. The spiritual aspects are an under-recognized and under-researched element of resilience, yet we find it interesting that, as you will see, all of the police officer narratives we will consider in this book contain some element of the spiritual dimension. It is an area that we have been researching for over ten years, and we will say more about the spiritual dimension in a later section in this Introduction.

Fitness

As Cornum (2012) shows, fitness is a key aspect of resilience. We look at the idea of fitness in our context here as an indication of a person's ability to cope effectively with the challenges of the leadership role – their resilience, as it were. Within many organizations, including the police, fitness is usually associated with *physical* fitness. Whilst this is certainly an important aspect, what Cornum and we refer to as "fitness" is a more holistic concept which includes physical, mental, and spiritual fitness.

Rayment and Smith (2013) have developed a useful framework called the Global Fitness Framework (GFF) to describe this holistic fitness, and we will link into this during some of the explorations in the text. In this section, we briefly explore this wider interpretation of fitness and draw on the GFF to look at its relevance for developing resilience.

Capra suggests that:

> *The more we study the major problems of our time, the more we come to realize that they cannot be understood in isolation. They are systemic problems, which means they are interconnected and interdependent ….*
> *There are solutions to the major problems of our time, some of them even simple. But they require a radical shift in our perceptions, our thinking, our values ….*
> (Capra 1997, cited in Kriger and Seng 2005: 773; our emphasis)

As we will discuss further in Chapter 9, the kind of systemic problem to which Capra refers highlights that we need to view resilience and its development in the same holistic way. This is not a new idea, and holistic approaches are regularly seen in healthcare, nursing, and leadership. Wilber (2001: 13), Covey (1999: 176) and Lips-Wiersma and Morris (2011b: 327) are four of the many advocates of this approach. The holistic approach recognizes that there are many aspects of resilience, and these are connected and interdependent, so you cannot explore or develop one aspect without impacting on others.

Using a holistic framework such as the GFF can also remind you to look at all areas, and not forget one.

The GFF shown in Figure 1.4 is a framework developed by Rayment and Smith (2013) that can be used not just to explore resilience, but a range of issues relevant to leadership demands today. In Figure 1.4, Rayment and Smith (2013: 5) use the term "organic level" to describe whether an individual, group, or society is being considered; "fitness plane" considers the strength, stamina, and suppleness of these levels, and "holistic depth" the physical, mental, and spiritual attributes being considered. Thus, each of the three aspects has three elements, giving a total of 27 individual cells. All of these individual cells are important in developing effective resilience, as is the connection between these and the overall approach. These 27 cells and all the different interconnections between them remind us of the complexity of the issues we are exploring here and shows there are no quick fixes or easy solutions.

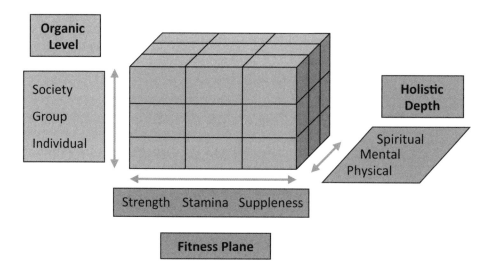

Figure 1.4   The Global Fitness Framework
Source: Rayment and Smith (2013: 5).

ORGANIC LEVEL

This level relates to whether an individual, group, or society is the focus of attention. Resilience is often only considered at an individual level, but the GFF draws our attention, as we shall see in this book, to the fact that there are many group, organizational, and societal factors that can have an impact and need to be considered.

FITNESS PLANE

The GFF encourages leaders to consider the fitness for purpose of individuals, groups, and societies. Fitness relates to an entity's ability to carry out its objectives or purpose. It is often considered in terms of strength, stamina, and suppleness: strength being the power that can be applied to a task, stamina the ability to sustain application of that power, and suppleness the ability to bend and flow, or to resist power in various ways. People are more familiar with these terms in relation to physical fitness, but Rayment and Smith (2013: 10) argue that they are also relevant to the study of mental and spiritual fitness, as we will discuss further in the next section.

An important aspect of resilience that is highlighted in the GFF is physical fitness. A range of research studies have highlighted the benefits of physical exercise on our ability to cope with stress, and certainly the majority of operational police officers work hard on their physical fitness in order to be able to cope with the demands of the job. Hills (2012: 14), focusing on physical fitness, claims that fitter employees are as much as 15 per cent more productive. This figure is significant, but we argue that the impact on productivity would be much higher if we focused on all the aspects of holistic fitness, as we are discussing here.

Wilson and Ferch (2005) emphasize the qualities of mental flexibility and being holistic when they talk about resilience: "[Resilience] refers to our ability to create and reintegrate new structures of thinking and behaving that provide us a more mature sense of coherence." This draws out the important suppleness element in the GFF. However, suppleness does not on its own effectively describe resilience. You need to be strong, supple, and have stamina to be resilient in a police or leadership role today, and it is the balance between these elements that is important. You can be too strong, for example, and not be supple enough, in which case you would not be very resilient. A piece of concrete for instance, may be very strong in compression and can withstand a lot of compacting pressure, but hard knocks can chip pieces off it, and once it is chipped it, stays chipped.

HOLISTIC DEPTH

This considers an entity's physical, mental, and spiritual aspects. Following Goleman's (2005) work on Emotional Intelligence, many would include emotions as a fourth section of the GFF. Emotions are certainly an important consideration, as we have highlighted earlier, but Rayment and Smith (2013: 27) argue that they can best be considered as two separate elements – short-term and long-term – and that both are contained within the GFF. Our emotions are displayed, and we work with them, through our physical, mental, and spiritual states. As an example, conflict can often cause strong emotional feelings that can result in an initial physical or mental over-reaction – "amygdala hijack" (Goleman, cited in Freedman 2002). Short-term emotions help individuals initiate the "fight or flight" response that may be necessary for survival. However, such extreme feelings tend to be short-lived, with more considered cognitive thoughts taking over once there has been sufficient time to reflect upon the incident's meaning and importance. Rayment and Smith (2013: 27) argue that the long-term aspects of emotions, such as love, faith, determination, and fear, are part of the spiritual dimension, while short-term emotions and their handling depend on the entity's physical, mental, and spiritual abilities. From this viewpoint, Emotional Intelligence may in part reflect the mental process by which we handle the short-term physical aspects of emotions and make long-term adjustments to our spiritual identity.

As we pointed out earlier, resilience is often considered as emotional resilience, or physical, or mental. The GFF is useful again in highlighting that whilst all these elements are important, there is a key aspect missing: that of the spiritual dimension. It is also the holistic interplay between all three elements that we need to consider.

The spiritual dimension is certainly the least understood, most contentious, and most often avoided aspect of leadership – and of the framework – and is rarely considered in explorations of resilience. We argue, however, that it is a key factor today, and much of our research has been in this area. We do not intend to explore the spiritual dimension in great depth in this Introduction, and we will return to it many times through the narratives of the police officers. However, a brief introduction to the concept will be useful, and this is the purpose of the next section.

Spirituality

Smith and Charles (2010) argue that many of the deeper issues related to the challenges that have been discussed earlier in this Introduction have a spiritual component to them. There is a growing awareness of this spiritual component within leadership studies, but although it is an important area that is vital for fitness and wellbeing, it is still an all too often unrecognized, unspoken, or unaddressed aspect of police work and leadership.

However, spirituality is a complex and contentious issue. Bouckaert and Zsolnai (2011: 6) are right to point out that spirituality cannot be captured in one definition because it is a "rich, intercultural and multilayered concept". In many organizations, including the police, it is important to recognize this complex intercultural nature and embrace as broad an interpretation of spirituality as possible, both in order to welcome the full breadth of the spiritual dimension – religious and non-religious – and also to allay fears of exclusion or discrimination, which can be one of the most significant concerns for people exploring the relevance of spirituality in an organizational context. Fry, for example, argues: "A key reason for excluding questions of workplace spirituality from leadership and other theories of management practice to date appears to be due to the confusion and confounding surrounding the distinction between religion and spirituality" (Fry 2003: 705).

In our explorations of the spiritual dimension with both police officers and leaders, we adopt a broad interpretation of "spiritual". As an example of this, Smith (2005) defines spirituality as: "a state or experience that can provide individuals with direction or meaning, or provide feelings of understanding, support, inner wholeness or connectedness. Connectedness can be to themselves, other people, nature, the universe, a god, or some other supernatural power."

Two key aspects to how we see spirituality are evident in this definition, which are explored further in Chapter 13. The first relates to meaning and purpose, and the second to various forms of connection. A more detailed exploration of the many different aspects to the spiritual dimension, and which links these to the Global Fitness Framework can be found in Smith and Rayment (2007).

Rothberg also provides a broad definition of spirituality that is another example of how we see spirituality and which seems applicable to policing and to leadership:

[Spirituality] involves doctrines and practices that help facilitate lived transformations of self and community toward fuller alignment with or expressions of what is "sacred". Such transformation typically occurs through the cultivation of qualities such as love and compassion, wisdom and deep understanding of the human condition, ethical integrity, personal and social liberation, harmony, and justice.

(Rothberg 1993: 105)

Despite the huge challenges and threatening nature of much of police work, you will see in the narratives from the police officers in the following chapters many instances of "love and compassion, wisdom and deep understanding of the human condition, ethical integrity, personal and social liberation, harmony, and justice", as described in the above definition. No doubt in your life and your leadership role you see many instances of these as well.

From Rothberg's definition, the phrase "a fuller alignment with or expression of what is sacred" is particularly interesting. In the large number of in-depth interviews we have conducted with police officers, we have seen a wide variety of interpretations of what they describe as sacred. What do you see as sacred? Why would you want to align more fully with this? How can you align your activities more fully, or express what is sacred? How would you do this, and how would developing a greater level of resilience assist you in this quest?

There is a great deal to the spiritual dimension, and our intention in this book is not to theorize too much about this or any of the other concepts we are exploring. This Introduction simply aims to briefly introduce the concept, and in the following chapters we let the practical narratives of police officers speak further about this important area of holistic fitness and resilience.

The Authors

The authors have both worked within the police environment in the USA and in the UK, as well as in management, training, and development. For over ten years they have been observing, researching, and testing ways in which police officers and leaders cope with the extremely challenging nature of their roles.[2]

---

2   You can find more details of this work on our website at http://www.policeresilience.com.

The authors bring very different perspectives and styles to this analysis: one is currently a police officer, the other an academic; one has a psychology background, the other is from business and education; one is male, the other female; one from the UK, the other from the USA. Their experiences and different perspectives provide both breadth and robustness to the ideas in this book. Their different styles will appeal to and engage different people. This breadth and robustness is further expanded by the different chapter authors – all police officers – who are or have been from different levels within the organizational hierarchy and have a variety of cultural perspectives. They have also contributed widely to the analysis sections. We offer our gratitude for their enormous and most valuable contributions.

The Book's Structure

The book is made up of 16 chapters. This Introduction and the Conclusions in the final chapter are separated by seven distinct parts. Each part consists of two chapters: the first chapter in each part is a detailed account from a police officer of a policing experience they have had. We give the police officers a voice here: the chapters are written by the police officers themselves, are in their own words, and discuss the issues they feel are important within that experience as well as what they think are important elements in how they coped with the crisis, event, or experience. As you read these, consider what is said and how it is said, but also what is not said in these narratives, because that can often be as important and reveal as much about that officer's ways of coping and resilience as anything else.

The second chapter in each part will then discuss the narrative and seek to draw out some insights, questions, and issues it raises with regard to resilience and how leaders might cope with particular aspects of their roles. Seven very different and challenging experiences are used in the book, from police officers across the world. We therefore hope that the learning from these will be applicable and relevant to many styles and levels of leadership and cultures internationally.

It is our intention to provide you, the reader, with stories and concepts that generate more questions for you and your self-reflection. It is not our intention to provide you with a framework or answers, but rather to offer assistance for your probing into what you may find helpful in keeping yourself resilient in your life and work in these challenging times.

In the final chapter we draw the exploration together and summarize the key points about resilience in leadership positions that we feel the narratives highlight. In keeping with the theme of the book, we present this is in a slightly unusual way, as a discussion between the two book authors. We hope you enjoy this and find it useful.

Case 1

2

Peak Experience at Gunpoint

Ginger Charles

Police work provides many opportunities and experiences to realign with importance of self, of family, of what is truly important. If not careful, police work can be as seductive as a mistress, leading one away from what is real and true in one's life. However, through the experience I recount in this chapter, I came to understand a sense of peace beyond what I had known before and an overwhelming love through transcending the crises in police work.

Prior to this experience, I was a police officer at another agency in a small Colorado mountain town for ten years. Throughout those years I remember having to "prove" myself in police work daily. It is an unwritten rule in police work that men need to prove themselves only once as a police officer. Women must prove themselves each shift. Every woman in police work knows this.

I was the only woman in the police department in this small town. It felt like I had 15 older brothers who were there to show me how to do the job. I was lucky they thought I was worthy of the attention. I worked very hard to show them I could do the job, be an effective police officer, and make them proud.

During my beginning years in police work, there was the informal hazing that can be common to new officers and female officers (informal hazing is group harassment, typically involving older members initiating newer members into the group). I remember being placed in the back seat of a patrol car and locked in. I was told to get myself out, which I did. I was locked in an evidence locker and told to figure my way out. Obviously, I was successful. My first day on the job, I was told by one of my sergeants, "Don't let us catch you putting makeup on while you're here at work."

These hazing behaviors were never viewed as malicious or vindictive, but rather an informal way of introducing me into the police work of men. I didn't know any better. Strangely, I knew they cared at some level. I still do not view the experience as harsh. However, I would never introduce another officer to the police world in this manner.

As a young officer, I often felt there was "something" larger than self and that I was being taken care of in those critical moments. Not that I didn't train or prepare for crises, it was more an understanding there was something more. I never considered myself religious, but rather spiritual. I had never been baptized and my father was an atheist, at best an agnostic. My mother was a firm believer in God and tried several churches. For me, I just knew there was something larger than me.

There were several times when I recognized I was in danger and things "worked out." My fellow police officers would tell me that it was police intuition that protects us; that we just know what to look out and watch for. Through training and experience, there are subtle cues we pay attention to as police officers, but I always knew there was something more. We certainly didn't talk about inner beliefs or feelings. There were times when I was the only police officer working in the entire county during a night shift. It was imperative to me that I had to have faith that I was watched over.

I would often ask for help from "God" or whatever was out there. I would pray for peace, for the courage to handle whatever I was dispatched to, make the best decision for myself and all involved. It seemed that my prayers were granted through my career. However, I was always very prepared to fight to the end and to lose my life if that was in the plans. I believed it was such an important profession, I felt I was in the right place.

There have been several experiences that I would call extraordinary—events beyond description. However, there is one experience that clearly represents my time in police work. The experience described here is not unique, but an example of what I have encountered several times during my career in police work.

The experience is beyond the phenomena of time and space. In fact, one may think a person is crazy for having the experience. However, I feel all the richer for the moment. In fact, I never spoke of the experience until well into my doctoral program, and then only with those who I thought would be open to hear it. I now leave it to you to judge.

Having ten years in police work, I decided to leave the small police department and work at a larger agency. There was the promise of more opportunities and challenges in this agency. I had already attained the rank of sergeant. But a move to another police department would require that I start over in my field as a police officer, patrolling the streets and answering calls at one of the larger police departments in the state of Colorado.

On a Saturday morning in February 2001, I was assigned to respond to a "disturbance" involving several Hispanic males in a parking lot connected to an apartment complex. Interestingly, the call was dispatched at 9:11 a.m., signifying "emergency." I was close to the location of the call and arrived within a minute of being dispatched. As I drove into the parking lot, the communication center "toned out" the call. A "toned out" call is an alert that signals to police officers a serious crime is occurring, such as a deadly force assault that is in progress. There is a significant adrenalin rush when an officer hears the tone. The alert tone was for me that day, the dispatcher then informing me that this call involved someone being "stabbed" at that location.

For some reason, no other police officers were close to the call and most of them were on the opposite side of the city. As I approached the scene, I saw a large Jeep-type vehicle (SUV) at the end of the parking lot. The vehicle had running boards along the side of the vehicle and there were at least four males standing on the running boards hitting people inside the SUV. At the time, I didn't see anyone with a knife, but knew I was in an "armed encounter" or deadly force assault.

I stopped my patrol car and jumped out, pulling my gun and pointing it at all the people in and around the vehicle. I was in between my patrol car door and the vehicle. This is normally a high-stress and fearful situation for a police officer. However, I did not feel any fear or apprehension. I was just responding to the call. Perhaps there was no sense of fear because of how quickly the call unfolded. I didn't have time to react or panic, but rather just responded through my training to the call as it played out.

Everyone appeared to be bleeding and I didn't know who had been stabbed. I didn't know who were the "bad" guys or the "good" guys when I drove up and there was no judgment from me. I just had to stop the fight. I immediately yelled for everyone involved to get down on the ground. It seemed like there was a constant flow of people coming out of the vehicle. One of the males ran from the area toward the apartment complex, leaving seven other people in the parking lot in front of me. I wasn't sure at that point whether the male was just running away or whether his intention was to run through the apartment complex and approach me from behind.

The apartments were on my left. It was a three-story building that had a walkway that went from where I was by my patrol car to the opposite side of the building, right where the first male had run. The other people and the big SUV were in front of my patrol car and the building in an open parking lot. Now that I think about it, I don't think there was one other car in the lot but that SUV.

I radioed to my dispatch center that I had "seven at gunpoint" and needed backup. I also told the dispatcher that one male had run from me into the adjoining apartment building. Five of the people complied with my orders to get down on the ground. However, two of the males started to challenge me, walking toward me as I yelled at them to get down on the ground.

I still didn't know who had a knife, who was injured, and where the one male who ran toward the apartment complex was. He had run toward the apartment building, possibly inside an apartment or in one of the many stairwells. I didn't know where he was. He also could have circled around the building to attack me from behind.

Police officers think tactically, so I was clearly aware that I was in a large parking lot with these other people. There was this large apartment complex on my left side and I was in an area that is not friendly toward police officers. There were two other males challenging me, five other people in front of me, one male somewhere off to my left, and no backup. Needless to say, I was in a tactically poor situation.

However, there is something unique that happens in crisis, at least for me. Time seems to stand still. What is interesting is the notion of "time standing still" and the "time" to think things through. I have asked other police officers whether they have experienced this alteration of time. Almost all have agreed that time seems to slow down or speed up. For me, it stood still.

The two males who started to walk toward me were coming from both my right and left, diverting my attention between the two of them—again a tactically poor situation. The five other individuals were still on the ground directly in front of me. They began to yell at the other two males to get down on the ground, that I was going to shoot them. They clearly recognized the dangerous situation we all were in at the moment.

One of the males screamed, "Get that fucking gun out of my face!" and the other male yelled, "You're not going to shoot me!" I repeated loud commands that I would shoot, to get on the ground, to comply. They continued to approach, and were approximately 15 feet from me when I experienced something beyond time and space.

I was very aware of what was occurring and I was also cognizant of the danger we all were in together. However, even though I heard myself yelling commands, heard the taunting and screaming from the approaching males, and saw and heard the other five people shouting at the two males, there was no fear or emotion. I seemed to have no judgment around this situation, nor any sense of time or space.

I remember looking at both males and calmly evaluating how close they could come before I would shoot them. As the event continued, I could picture the two males walking closer and I saw in my mind, shooting my gun and the exact location of my bullet strikes on both males. I saw myself shoot the male on the left twice in the chest. I saw him fall; the bullets passed through his body and into the dirt behind him. I saw myself then shoot the male on the right. I shot him in the chest and head, the bullets also exiting his body and landing in the dirt beyond him.

I recognized in my mind this would be considered a "good shooting" from those (attorneys, police, and so on) critiquing my actions years from now. I was comfortable with the possibility of needing to shoot them. Police officers are told from the first day on the job to think about having to shoot their gun, possibly having to kill someone. It is important to resolve this possibility or probability in their minds because once you are in a deadly force encounter, it is too late to think about whether you can kill someone.

However, I was not alone in this situation. There were eight of us involved and all of our actions were important. I felt an immense presence and understanding of unconditional choice for each individual in this scene. I also was aware of the precariousness of the situation as well as a strange beauty of the encounter. More on this later.

I felt as if we were all inside a bubble of "protection" where there was nothing more important for us than this moment. Together, we would or could choose how the remainder of the scene played out. We were dependent on each other's choices and actions, and those actions were probably irreversible.

Suddenly, I could see a blackboard cross in front of my field of vision in my mind's eye. It never blocked my view, but was part of the scene now. I could see something being written in cursive on the board by an unknown hand. While all this was happening, I was still challenging the males, they were continuing to walk toward me, and the others were still yelling at the two males.

There was one word written on the board in front of me. It was "PRECLUSION." For those not familiar with the word, in my world it means recognizing that you have exhausted all levels of control prior to the use of deadly force. Without thinking, I pulled my canister of "pepper spray," sometimes mistakenly called "mace," from my duty belt and held it under my extended gun. Again, this was happening as I continued to yell at the males walking toward me. In fact, all of us were yelling.

Mace is a chemical spray used by law enforcement and the military. It is sprayed into the face of the suspect and it burns, irritating the mucus membranes in the nose, mouth, and eyes. When I pulled the canister, the two males immediately fell to the ground almost simultaneously. I was stunned. I am sure I had a very stupid look on my face, perhaps amazement. I didn't spray them, but they began to beg, "Don't Mace me, don't Mace me!" What did these guys think, that I wouldn't shoot them? At that moment, my first backup officer arrived. Three minutes had now passed since I was first dispatched to this call.

The entire event felt strange and unique, weird and wondrous. I did not share it with my fellow police officers. I kept it my secret until it became a part of me and the police officer I was becoming. It was the beginning of my inquiry into spirituality of police work. It was also the true beginning of my research in my doctoral program.

The call ended with the males arrested for not complying with police orders. One of the males had a warrant for his arrest for murder of a police officer in another jurisdiction. They were both drunk and lucky to be alive. I often wondered why I didn't shoot. However, one of the males approached me after the scene was secured and said, "Thanks for not killing me." I was able to tell him, "You're welcome," and truly mean it.

What is interesting is that while the experience was unusual, this is a typical call for service in police work. After responding to this situation, I had other calls for service throughout my shift. I continued my day without much thought about what had occurred. I know I thought about the experience quite a bit when reflecting on my own time. However, I did not think about it during my shift.

Sometimes we, as police officers, can feel very separate from those we serve in the community. We are often frustrated with people and their poor choices that bring us to them. I felt none of that frustration with these individuals. There was a sense of connection with them. Yet today I have no idea where they are or what they are doing. It was a moment together where I was given an opportunity to learn from them.

I can remember this scene as if it happened yesterday. I currently live very close to the original scene and often walk by the parking lot. In thinking about this years later, I am clear this time was given to me to show me how important we are to each other, no matter the role we play. Whether it's cops and crooks or something else, we are here together to come to the highest good for all involved. This moment in time felt like grace. It was sacred for me.

What I do not know is what effect it had on the other people involved in this with me. Perhaps I am not meant to know. I also wonder if they too were experiencing a shift in time and space. What was written on their blackboards? What did they learn?

Leader Reflection

- What stands out for you in this narrative regarding resilience?
- What elements of this narrative link to the aspects of resilience you are working with?
- What other elements of the narrative are important to you, and why?

3

Peak Experience at Gunpoint: Analysis

This chapter aims to discuss Ginger's narrative in Chapter 2 and draw out issues that leaders in a wide variety of environments and work settings can learn from. We also suggest that police officers are leaders in their own right, so this learning can be applied to police officers as well as leaders in other work environments.

As we have highlighted in the Introduction, what is apparent in policing is the confrontation with crises on a daily basis. Often police officers encounter situations that leaders in other public and private sector organizations do not. The central argument in this text, however, is that while the situation experienced by a leader may not be as pronounced or extreme as that experienced by the police officer, there are many similar things that leaders in other organizations experience. Because policing magnifies the issues, they are often easier to see and understand.

We believe this is very much the case with Ginger's narrative. This is a powerful and profound experience, and as we will see, there are some important points with regard to resilience that we can draw from this experience. Although there are many themes that emerge within Chapter 2, we intend to focus on just a few. We encourage you to consider additional areas that reveal themselves to you. It is the goal of the book to allow you to interpret what is most important for you in each chapter while the authors outline some of the predominant themes with respect to building resilience.

Peak Experience

One of the important and interesting concepts in this narrative is Ginger's use of the words "peak experience". When one begins to think about an experience of life or death, of confronting several individuals with at least two of them wanting to hurt/kill what is in front of them, and hoping to survive, it seems to be quite an imperative that one operates in a "peak" state of mind.

Maslow is well known for his work on peak experiences, and found from his research into peak experience that: "all or almost all people have or can have peak-experiences" and "in the peak experience the nature of reality may be seen more clearly and its essence penetrated more profoundly" (Maslow 1994: 29).

Maslow also describes individuals who experience many "peak" moments as being *self-actualized*. Self-actualized people are those operating at the top of Maslow's well-known hierarchy (Maslow 1968). He suggests that self-actualized people are generally not confused about right and wrong, and make ethical decisions more quickly and more surely than average people (Smith 2005: 95).

Maslow defines self-actualization as:

> *an episode, or a spurt in which the powers of the person come together in a particularly efficient and intensely enjoyable way, and in which he [sic] is more integrated and less split, more open for experience, more idiosyncratic, more perfectly expressive or spontaneous, or fully functioning, more creative, more humorous, more ego-transcending, more independent of his lower needs, etc. He becomes in these episodes more truly himself, more perfectly actualising his potentialities closer to the core of his Being, more fully human.*
>
> *(Maslow 1968:97)*

Some of the characteristics of self-actualized people Maslow identified may be summarized as:

1.   superior perception of reality;

2.   increased spontaneity;

3.   increased acceptance of self and others, or

4.   increased detachment and desire for privacy;

5.   greatly increased creativity;

6.   increased identification with the human species;

7.   increased autonomy and resistance to enculturation;

8.   higher frequency of peak experiences;

9.   an increase in problem-centring;

10.   improved interpersonal relations.

If we explore the above list, it appears that a number of the characteristics outlined are described in Ginger's narrative, particularly characteristics 1–7. Certainly her perception of reality (characteristic 1) was intense, as this was a life or death incident. The necessity for spontaneity (characteristic 2) was apparent as the scene was evolving and dynamic. She describes her responses as "fluid and intuitive".

Also evident is the absence of judgement (characteristic 3) as to whether the situation was "good or bad" as she is confronted by these angry men and women. She says she feels no fear or judgement about the situation. There is no condemnation from Ginger as she negotiates with the individuals to gain compliance. It could be said that she is detached from the emotions in the event (characteristic 4). This detachment also seems to extend to the after-events, as she did not share her feelings or beliefs with her co-workers and chose to reflect on them in her own time.

Her acceptance of self and the other people in the event seems to have given her the advantage of increasing her creativity whilst still in the experience (characteristic 5). She is able to move beyond any judgement or personal attachment of roles in the experience. She speaks of an appreciation for the human beings involved with her during the experience (characteristic 6). This appears to have provided her an opportunity to think creatively without "freezing" her responses to violence.

Much of what we see on the nightly news with regard to bad police decisions most likely began with an officer taking the situation personally or from an egocentric position, centred on themselves rather than others. From this position, the danger then is that the officer cannot think clearly through his or her perceptions of the situation, which will always "colour" the outcome. Many officer-involved injuries and injuries to suspects are the result of not thinking clearly through all possible scenarios. The "self" gets in the way, and the consequences are not thought out beyond the individual.

As leaders, it may be useful to remember that it is the "behaviour" of our difficult employees that is the issue, not the employees themselves. Again, it is the behaviour we wish to affect or influence, it is not the employee we should want to change. How can we best function in whatever situation or crisis we encounter with the highest intentions for the consumer, employee, and community? Stepping out of our ego can provide us with a clearer view of what is actually occurring, rather than imposing our own views and beliefs, particularly when leaders are faced with the demands of working with various individuals with a variety of issues, talents, and concerns.

So many of the comments in Ginger's narrative would seem to suggest that she is operating at the self-actualized level in Maslow's hierarchy. The above list also highlights that self-actualized people experience a higher frequency of peak experiences (characteristic 8). It certainly seems that operating at a peak state at that apartment complex on that Saturday morning back in February 2001 assisted Ginger.

Based on the characteristics identified above, we would argue that people who are operating at the self-actualized level are more resilient individuals. What do you think? Have you ever had a peak experience, and if so, do you feel it enabled you to cope more effectively with the situation you were experiencing then?

Emotions

Ginger describes in the narrative her recognition of the emotions of the group she is dealing with. She hears the shouts and yells from the people complying as well as the two males who were challenging her. It is apparent that she is able to detach herself from her emotions, and her feeling of detachment allows her to move beyond the emotions to get to the resolution of the immediate problem. In this situation, her ability to look past the emotion seems to have created the space in the moment for all participants to work toward a solution. This is a clear example of Emotional Intelligence (EQ), which we will explore further in Chapter 7.

With regard to emotions, it is sometimes easy for leaders to become overly involved in details, putting aside any emotions and forgetting about the human being behind the details. Conversely, leaders may become overly involved in the human being, forgetting the details. Maintaining an appropriate balance is the key. When leading people, the recognition of how we are affecting others around us is imperative to our importance as leaders. People who work for us give us the opportunity to "control" or influence them. It is the same for a police officer who is "given" authority to "control" the community members.

How do you as a leader approach conflict and emotions? Do you feel you maintain an appropriate balance in dealing with the emotions involved in the situations you face?

We explore more on emotions and Emotional Intelligence in Chapter 7 because we believe, like Gilmartin (2002), that emotions and the effective management of them are key elements to building resilience.

Time

Ginger suggests in her narrative that she and other police officers have found that time can either slow down or speed up in conflict or critical situations. Indeed, Ginger experienced time almost coming to a standstill on that Saturday morning at the apartment complex. It also seems that so much occurred during that time even though the entire scenario was completed in just three minutes. Have you ever had experiences like this? What is the significance of this for you?

As Ginger was immersed in the experience, she was not aware of any time limitations or deadlines. She was only aware of the situation. The importance of this awareness seemed to provide an opening or opportunity to allow the situation to unfold. Often, as leaders, we may feel forced to get the job done by a certain deadline, focused on quantity rather than the quality of the experience. This may have a number of positive outcomes. What do you feel they are? Can you identify any difficulties with this time-driven focus?

Athletes have often portrayed this perceptual distortion of time as being "in the zone". This particular mindset then provides an opening for the athlete to surge ahead of the others towards victory. In fact, as outlined by Harung et al. (2009) athletes may often describe their performance as moving at a normal speed while they watch their competition move in slow motion.

Another example of this time distortion has been described by those individuals practising Transcendental Meditation (TM) (Travis et al. 2002). Those practising TM describe that there is space where time is not important or acknowledged. They are aware of their surroundings, but do not feel attached to anything. Many TM participants have suggested they are in another realm of space and time during their practice. In addition, this space has been described as "peaceful", "centred", "focused", and "objective" (Travis et al. 2002).

The sensation of time loss or gain offers leaders the chance to do the same. It seems that as these athletes, TM practitioners and Ginger focus on the task or game in front of them, they move into a state of timelessness to get the job done gracefully with the best possible outcomes. Certainly, there is a need for deadlines to accomplish some goals and projects. However, leaders who can move into a state of timelessness may themselves have a chance to focus on the experience and the best possible outcomes rather than on the concept of time. Have you ever done this? Could you? What are your fears, perceptions, or concerns that may be holding you back from achieving this? What might be the advantage if you could? How might this impact on your resilience?

Attention

Ginger describes her connection with the group, and seems to have a full awareness about what each person in the scenario is doing. The seven people in front of her have more immediacy than the one male who ran away towards the apartment building on her left. In a perfect scenario, she would have had backup officers to protect her should this one male come around behind her, but she did not. This need for awareness is also true for leaders. We must be paying attention to what is occurring in front of us as well as aware of what has escaped our view.

Ginger's narrative reminds us that to be resilient, leaders cannot do everything and need to prioritize their goals and objectives – paying attention to what is in front of us, letting go of those demands that may need to be handled at a later time, and recognizing the ones that can be left completely. Facing the most important issues that confront us is significant in our approach to the concept of time.

We frequently work with people who are simply trying to do too much. They may be able to survive doing this in the short term, but we argue that it is likely to have a knock-on effect on their health and resilience over the longer term. They need to prioritize. A useful tool which can assist people to prioritize is the "Important–Urgent" grid shown in Figure 3.1. This is a concept that was first introduced by Covey (1989). In this grid, "urgent" means something that you have to do right now, or as close to that as possible, whereas "important" are those tasks that will deliver something in terms of your personal values and goals.

Figure 3.1   A prioritizing grid

We can frequently find ourselves being drawn into the bottom right-hand box in Figure 3.1 – the "Not Important but Urgent" – when we need to be devoting more of our time to thinking about the top boxes, which contain the important aspects to our work and life.

You may find it useful to identify where the things you are working on now fit in Figure 3.1, and where you spend your time. How can you find more time to work in the top left-hand box in Figure 3.1, "Important but Not Urgent"?

Connection

One of the most fascinating perspectives in Ginger's narrative is her description of the connection she experienced with each subject. She is aware that some of the group's members appear to want to hurt her. Yet she remains open, choosing not to pigeon-hole anyone into a role in the situation, such as "suspect". Her objectivity remains clear as well. This ability to remain open and non-judgemental seems to be an important aspect of resilience. Rather than getting lost in anger, frustration, and emotions, and making biased, discriminatory, and inappropriate judgements which will all have to be justified objectively later and require a great deal of time and energy, she is able to remain open. This is a difficult balance, though, as police officers are required to make quick judgements all the time, (as we shall see later in some of the other narratives). It is the same for leaders. What do you think are the key elements to making appropriate judgements in the stressful situations you face? We will explore more on decision-making in Chapter 9.

In the current research within the police culture, many police officers describe their work as a "calling" (Charles 2009; Smith and Charles 2010). They recognize the need to push through where their own safety or lives are in danger. While there is recognition that they may be seriously injured or killed, the understanding is in selfless service of community. They have often described their beliefs of "something larger than self" beyond what they are experiencing. Police officers have also explained they are an instrument of God as they fight evil in their work.

A police officer in Charles' research gives a very practical example of how he was "called" to do the work of a police officer:

My mom had a baby when I was about 13 years old. Then my mom went to Kentucky for a while and left us in the housing projects. So my older sister and I raised my younger sister. Then we had another stepfather who entered our lives and he was an alcoholic. I remember one night, he was drunk as a skunk, and he was telling my older sister that when she went to sleep he was going to come into the bedroom and gouge out her eyes with a knife. I remember how scared we were, huddled together, and I thought, there must be a way to fix this for the victims. They [relationships] gave me a foundation of what's right and wrong and I thought I better get a job where I can help these kids who are huddled in the corner, afraid of their stepfather coming in their bedroom and gouging out their eyes.

(Charles 2005: 111)

This selfless service has clear links to the self-actualized level in Maslow's hierarchy we explored earlier, and can be described as a humanistic form of spirituality. Zohar and Drake (2000) identify the concept of Spiritual Intelligence (SQ), which is a progression from both Intelligence Quotient (IQ) and Emotional Intelligence. Zohar and Drake highlight a number of characteristics of spiritually intelligent people, and some of these we summarize as:

1. holistic – whole person, whole system;

2. self-aware – both reflective and self-confronting;

3. spontaneous – alive to the moment and not afraid to respond or initiate;

4. flexible – open to suggestion, surprise and change, and able to cope with ambiguity;

5. able to learn from adversity and turn bad experiences into wisdom;

6. able to reframe situations – new perspectives;

7. led by their own vision, values, and sense of purpose;

8. independent and willing to take a stand on issues;

9.   questioning – especially 'why' questions;

10.   welcoming of diversity.

These characteristics have many similarities to the characteristics of Maslow's self-actualized people we explored earlier. As well as feelings of connectedness, which link to characteristic 1, we also see characteristics 1–6 described in Ginger's narrative. Ginger is able to reframe this critical event into a new experience whereby she learns rather than blames the participants (characteristic 6). Her belief that they are all in the experience to learn and accept the best choice of action for all is considered as moving beyond self into a holistic approach of what is good for all in the situation, rather than the self (characteristic 1). Here she is clearly learning from the adverse event and finding deep wisdom from the experience (characteristic 5).

Extraordinary Experiences

In the narrative, Ginger talks about her reluctance to share her experience with others. She appears to find the experience beyond belief. However, she does eventually share the story because of how powerful the experience was to her growth: it was a life-changing moment for her. This is also the lesson. When leaders take the risk to tell what is closest to their hearts, disregarding the fear, they gain strength in the risk. They set an example to others to do the same. Bakan quotes Oscar Olivia, a union official who led a popular uprising against the privatization of the freshwater system in Cochamba, Bolivia, who said:

> We live in a world full of fear, people are afraid of the dark, people are afraid of giving their opinion, people are afraid of acting .... It's time that we lose that fear ... [and] develop the capacity to unite, to organise, and to recover our faith in ourselves and in others.
>
> (Bakan 2005: 164)

Maybe it is time for us all to lose the fear and recover our faith in ourselves and others.

The risk Ginger takes in talking about and sharing her experiences can provide opportunities for new learning and for opening ourselves to others. Here is another example of what this peak experience offers. When we as leaders take a chance to share from our hearts and souls, we open ourselves to other extraordinary experiences.

The act of telling our stories appears to have faded from importance in society. Yet there are many lessons in the hearing of each others' stories. In the telling of our stories, the listener is brought closer to the person telling the story. By opening our hearts to each other, we become clearer in our messages to each other. The listener finds their own meaning in another's story, and then may take the risk to tell their own story. All lives become enriched through the sharing. There is less distance between us when we share our moments – and we all have these moments.

This distance, constructed by race, creed, gender, and so on, only produces more violence. When we distance ourselves, we can criticize or condemn each other, failing to recognize the humanness in each of us. This behaviour only promotes further distance and a de-valuing of each individual, culture, community, or organization.

You may find yourself remembering a moment that was so powerful but incredible that you find it difficult to share and may never have shared it. What do you do with the experiences that are beyond your belief? How can we find meaning and purpose in these stories? If we choose to ignore these experiences, what do we lose? We would suggest that we lose richness in our lives. Have you ever had what you would describe as an extraordinary experience? If so, have you shared this with others? Who did you share it with, and why them? If you have not shared it, what prevents you doing this? What might be the benefits if you did share it?

Maslow suggests that these peak or extraordinary experiences can provide deep inspiration and value to the person's life. He writes, "the power of [one peak] experience could permanently affect the attitude towards life" (Maslow 1994: 75).

You Are Not Alone

Another powerful aspect in this narrative is that it shows that although Ginger did not have any backup initially to support her on that Saturday morning in the apartment complex, she was not alone. Someone/something else was there to offer the blackboard she saw with the word "PRECLUSION" on it.

We believe, particularly in times of difficulty and extreme stress, that someone is there to guide you. This offers us tremendous resilience.

Conclusion

Most leaders may not be faced with life or death situations. However, we will always have an effect on others with our choices. Sometimes leaders' choices dramatically affect the individuals around them. Whether giving a presentation or conducting training, responding to a difficult situation or implementing a particular organizational strategy that has been imposed, we as leaders are required to make difficult decisions that affect those around us all the time. As effective leaders, we are and remain aware of our people and their needs. We make decisions that best reflect as many needs as possible. The less we are attached to the outcomes, the clearer the decisions. If we become observers of facts, we can enter the "zone" or a peak performance and flow with the situation, allowing information to move to us and through us, resolving conflict and building relational strengths in our people. This provides the opportunity for selfless service in our work, and can provide us with vast untapped reserves of resilience.

Ginger's experience demonstrates a true relational moment whereby the entire group has an opportunity to make a choice. Each individual has a responsibility and a consequence in the event. Each person is valued in their choice – the group accepted the consequences, and were all dependent upon others' choices.

Case 2

4

Hurricane Katrina—a Police Officer's Experience

Wendy Kipple[1]

I started my career in police work by answering an ad in the local newspaper. I was a horse trainer, but the work had become unsteady in the economy. When I saw the ad, I thought, "I can do this," and I became a cop.

As I grew into the job, I became more and more fascinated with the investigations side of law enforcement and took several classes. I was also interested in death investigation and began an ancillary assignment as a coroner's investigator. My work in death investigations was the foundation of my calling as a police officer because it became my mission to give the dead the last bit of dignity I could as they left this world.

My experiences in New Orleans after Hurricane Katrina only served to enforce my beliefs in the importance of my mission. What I journaled during my time there is still as powerful today as it was when it occurred. I can read what I wrote then and immediately return to those days in my mind. I hope readers find my words as meaningful as I do.

Colorado

Today is the beginning of a test of what I have learned in all the training exercises over the past three years as a member of the Disaster Mortuary Response Team (DMORT). We are responding to New Orleans, Louisiana, to help pick up the pieces in the wake of Hurricane Katrina. I am not quite sure what to expect or what I will be doing, but I feel like I am up for the challenge.

---

1   Edited from the journal of Wendy Kipple.

Yesterday afternoon my Team Commander called me and requested that I start calling team members here in Colorado to see who could leave for Louisiana first thing the next morning. It took me a couple of hours, but I was multitasking like crazy!

I changed my voicemail as I readied myself for packing. As I left my lab and office at the police department, I turned around and took one last look at my familiar world, turned out the light, closed the door, and began. We were told to expect to be gone for two to three weeks and to pack accordingly, but as light as possible.

We were also told to bring our own bedding, toilet paper, and towels. We were to meet at the Houston Airport and rent vehicles to drive to Baton Rouge. I flew from Denver to Houston, arrived around 4:30 p.m. and met six other Region 8 DMORT members. We were given a van, a team fuel card, and told to contact our Team Commander upon our arrival. When we walked outside to the van, someone handed me the keys and said, "You're a cop, we elect you to drive." I was a bit intimidated, but drove the entire six hours from Texas to Baton Rouge, Louisiana.

En route, we saw bus after busload of people being taken from New Orleans to the Astrodome stadium in Houston. Every rest area was filled with cars and buses, obviously victims of the hurricane. The closer we got to Baton Rouge, the less vehicles that were going in our direction.

New Orleans

I am told that tomorrow we will be starting body recovery in New Orleans. I wish I could sleep. I only slept four hours last night, fitfully because I was so wired about coming here to do a job that I have been training for.

It is the next day and we are waiting for our commanders to find out what and where our assignments will be. Things in New Orleans are really bad, with looters attacking and shooting at rescue workers. As a law enforcement officer, it makes me feel vulnerable to be here where rescue workers are being attacked and shot at, and my vest and gun are sitting in my locker at my police department in Colorado. Right now I am regretting my decision to leave my vest and gun there.

Currently my task here is to help one of the DMORT Commanders with supply and equipment acquisitions for the team. I realized that I am currently one of two fingerprint specialists here and I heard that there are 200,000 people missing and maybe 10,000 dead! It sounds like we are going to be busy.

Right behind the Management Support Team Center, there is a critical care triage unit with medical evacuation helicopters landing and taking off one right after the other, without ceasing. Around 6:30 p.m., I was taken to the Disaster Portable Morgue Unit, which is a 200,000 square foot warehouse located 13 miles south of Baton Rouge. Our command offices and housing will be in the classrooms of an old run-down high school adjacent to the warehouse. We planned to set up our cots in the gymnasium, but realized the roof was gone. Instead, we ate cold beans and rice and then set up in classrooms, which were stacked from floor to ceiling with furniture and broken equipment.

The heat and humidity here are brutal. I am sweating like never before. There are old air conditioning units that will require a bit of work to get them functioning again. The bathrooms haven't been used in so long that they are barely functional. A couple of guys figured a way to run a garden hose from the janitor's closet so we can shower. We hung a tarpaulin down the middle of one classroom to create separate spaces for men and women to sleep.

Today is another day of organized chaos. We were divided into two strike teams to drive into New Orleans and pick up bodies. We got a report that there are 250 bodies at the Superdome sports stadium. Water is still about two feet high all around the Superdome. When we arrived, the stench was overwhelming but we found only one body. Then we went to the airport and picked up nine bodies that were there and headed back to the morgue in St Gabriel. This place looks and feels like a war zone, and it's very eerie here in a major city devoid of normal life.

When we got back to the morgue, we moved the bodies into a refrigerated trailer to await processing through the morgue. The guys that are responsible for setting up the morgue had it all set up, but had to take it down when they realized that during the heat of the day the temperature was about 110°F inside! There was no way we would be able to work inside there with Tyvek suits (protective white overalls), gloves, and masks. So they took everything down and used six large tents. They got several huge air conditioning units that are the size of large storage sheds and then ran air ducts inside the tents.

I have been working 15 to 18 hours a day, even pulling a 36-hour day with 3½ hours of sleep snuck in here and there recently. What little down time I have is spent sleeping or calling family to let them know I am alright. Trying to get cell phone service here is quite challenging. It is difficult at best, and the calls get dropped about every 30 seconds.

We have a few minutes of silence each morning to remember the victims of this disaster. The Forest Service Support Team arrived from California and made our camp life considerably more comfortable. They brought in a huge trailer with 12 showers inside. They also brought in a large catering service and set up three big eating tents with rows of tables and chairs, just like a cafeteria. Another needed service they brought was a laundry service. Our camp population is about 300 people now with all the Forest Service staff, DMORT, and support staff.

I have now gone to New Orleans a couple of times to pick up bodies from certain locations. We went to one place in the city that was not so nice. We were waiting for our box truck to load the bodies and heard gunfire. We quickly realized that we were either a target or were in the same crossfire. We ran inside the building and took cover until our Army escorts told us it was clear. Now I am really regretting not bringing my gun and vest. I hate feeling this vulnerable and helpless without the tools of my trade to protect myself and others. Gangs and criminals are running rampant in New Orleans, with the criminals trying to take over the city. It just boggles my mind. Why are these people shooting at the people that are here to help them? The Federal Protective Service (FPS) officers that are arriving in large numbers are here to help police and provide protection. Their orders are to give two warnings to anyone they come across committing a crime or armed with a weapon. If they don't comply, they are to shoot them. Currently I have heard these officers have shot 66 people.

I just grabbed about an hour and a half of sleep and then got up to work as a body tracker in the morgue. I worked all night and then was volunteered to drive one of the 27 trailer rigs in the morning that would pull the 53-foot refrigerated trailers that were being used to store the bodies that had been recovered from central New Orleans. All of the bodies that we processed through the morgue the first night were from a nursing home that had not taken on any water, so there was little decomposition. What really sickened me was the shape that these elderly people were in. Most of them were very emaciated and had large angry bedsores that looked very painful. These people looked like starving people from Ethiopia. They lay in their body bags, mouths open as if screaming in agony, some of them still had their eyes open and looked as if they were pleading with us to help them. I prayed that each of them was now at peace and at least not in any pain any more.

Each body I was assigned would start off in the Admitting section. Next there was a team of four people (Forensic Anthropologist, Forensic Pathologists, and a scribe). Personal effects and clothing were removed and documented. The team would determine race and sex, examining the body in detail, to include scars, tattoos, and anything else that could be used for identification. I then took the body to the Photography and Personal Effects station. The body was photographed with any personal effects. The next station was the Fingerprint station, then the Dental station. The following station was a full-body X-ray, looking for prosthetics that could help us in identification. Most prosthetics or implants have a serial number that can be traced to the patient.

The DNA section involved removing a chunk of bone from the body's tibia that included a section of bone marrow. The marrow was placed in a tube and put in a freezer. If a full autopsy was required, then the body would move to that station. The final stop was the exit morgue, where the body was placed in a clean body bag, all paperwork associated with the body was in a plastic sleeve, and the body then put on the refrigerated trailer.

By 6 a.m. we had processed all the bodies currently at the morgue. I quickly went to get an hour and a half of sleep, got up, took a shower, and drank lots of coffee. Then we went and picked up three of the semi-tractors and traveled to New Orleans.

We were being escorted by an FPS officer through traffic and checkpoints. The trailers we were to hook up to were parked at the water's edge on the main highway, I-10. When I hooked up my rig, I then had to climb into the trailer to count the bodies. While I was standing there, I took a minute to look around. I was standing in the middle of I-10, which was deserted. There was a helicopter nearby that took off. The water was running and rolling around the interstate, black, stinking, and dirty. It smelled like nothing I had ever smelled before. I watched toys and personal possessions float by. It was strange to see a major city so devastated and devoid of life and activity.

My next assignment was with a strike team. Our first assignment was to respond to a big hospital that had a report of six bodies in the Intensive Care Unit (ICU). We had to wait to enter the hospital when we arrived because there was a pack of domesticated dogs that had become feral inside the hospital. The Federal Police had to respond to shoot them. That broke my heart.

When the coast was clear, we suited up in Tyvek suits, knee-high rubber boots, hinged face shields, and headlamps. I was certain there was no power inside the hospital. It was very eerie to be walking down the darkened hallways of a hospital that just a couple of weeks ago was brightly light, bustling with activity—now empty, quiet, and damaged.

Trash was everywhere and the stench was horrible. We were literally walking the halls doing the "sniff test" to find the bodies as they decomposed. When we reached the ICU unit on the 8th floor, it was dark except for the ambient light coming through the windows of the patient rooms. The overpowering smell of death greeted our noses as soon as we walked through the doors. What lay beyond the doors was worse than any Stephen King horror novel. We could hear respirators running and empty IV pumps beeping, but no other sound. Everything was running on backup battery power. It was very disturbing to see patients still hooked up to equipment when it was obvious they had been dead for quite some time. The bodies lay in their beds, bloated and decomposing, with bodily fluids in pools under and around the beds.

We disconnected the patients from their respirators and IVs, put them in body bags and carried them to the stairwell. We had a good team of people, professional and knowledgeable. We treated each body with respect and dignity. I had to wonder what their last hours were like. Why were they left to die alone? Were they conscious and aware that they were going to die alone? That really bothered me. We carried each body bag down the eight flights of stairs to another team and the waiting refrigerator trucks.

We then returned to the 5th floor and took a break after looking for more bodies, dumping water on our heads. The heat and humidity was stifling. After our break, we went down to the morgue and removed the bodies from the coolers. Some of them were already into advanced stages of decomposition. I remember I happened to look down and saw a pair of feet that were sticking out of the sheets covering the body. The feet had blue-green mold! These sights and smells will be forever ingrained in my memory.

We were told of two more bodies that needed to be recovered. One was a 14-year-old girl who had been tied to a fence by Search and Rescue workers. The other was a man tied to a tree. I was really bothered by the 14-year-old.

My own daughter is close to the same age. I wondered why this girl was out here alone. How did she become separated from her parents and family? Once we collected them, we traveled back to the morgue to be off the streets before the 6 p.m. curfew.

Some of the things I have seen come through are very odd, and you have to wonder what is going through people's minds as they are trying to escape their impending death. One guy today had two belts on, his cell phone clipped to one of the belts, a television remote in one front pants pocket, a power cord for some unknown electronic device, and what I finally figured out was a mud-encrusted roll of adding machine tape. I have even seen a couple of elderly people come in with life jackets on. It is interesting to see what different things trigger each individual's emotions while doing this kind of work. We have even seen some bodies come through that were already deceased before the hurricane and were embalmed, prepped, and dressed for their funeral.

Yesterday we processed 97 bodies through the morgue. We have a good working flow going, but were thorough and treated each victim with dignity and respect no matter their sex, race, or class. Today we only had 19 bodies to process and we got them through in just a few hours. We actually got it done with a skeleton crew (no pun intended), because we were advised that another hurricane is heading our direction and we had to move all the bodies, 500+ so far, from the freezer pods that were set up, back into the reefer trailers to prepare for possible evacuation. When we finished processing what few bodies we had, we went out and helped move and load bodies. When we were done, we went to get our medical check, which we had to do before and after our shifts. Several of us would always place bets on which of us had the lowest blood pressure. I always won that contest. I think it is because I live at such a high altitude, and being at such a low altitude and having more oxygen to breathe was to my advantage.

When we were done, we went to the shower trailer for a nice cold shower. I never in my life thought I would say that I enjoyed cold showers, but with the extreme heat and humidity here, it is very much a pleasant experience.

I only have tomorrow left here to work, and then I will travel to the airport in Baton Rouge by 6 a.m. on Thursday morning. It is hard to believe that I have been here for three weeks. It seems as if it has been an eternity. Yet I feel I am leaving right when things are rolling good. I have met some incredible people from all over the United States.

Something that one of the doctors stressed to us we will all go through when we return to our reality at home is that being deployed on a disaster is akin to going to war. She has been to several major disasters, such as the airline crash in Guam, the Walker County, Georgia crematorium incident, the Alaska air crash and the World Trade Center. So she has been through these experiences enough to know what to expect. She warned us that our family and friends back home will be happy and relieved to have us home, but we should not to expect anyone to be able to fully comprehend or understand the horrific things we have seen, heard, and even smelled here. I think she is right, because I can't even begin to find the words that can adequately describe exactly what each of us is going through here.

This same doctor also emphasized there will be triggers that will bring us back to this wretched place. All of us here have indirectly been through a traumatic event together and many of us will have developed bonds that will be strong lifelong friendships, and if any of us start to have any issues with our experiences here, we need to call and talk through it with each other. It is nice to know that there is that kind of support network among the DMORT members, although I don't particularly think that I am really going to have any difficulty with what I have experienced here.

I brought a variety of skills and knowledge here with me to do a difficult job, and it makes me feel good to have been able to help people out doing a job that most people don't even want to think about. I feel members of DMORT are kind of the unsung heroes of the National Disaster Medical System. No, we aren't out there in the forefront like DMAT (Disaster Medical Assist Team), making dramatic rescues and providing the necessary medical treatment for the living survivors of these tragedies, but we work quietly in the background, collecting the bodies of loved ones, working diligently to identify them, and hopefully send them home to their loved ones so that they may start the grieving process and have some closure.

I feel like I am coming home a much better person and have learned so much about just how deep I can dig inside myself and find the strength and stamina I didn't know I had to get a difficult job accomplished in the most professional manner possible. I have also learned an incredible amount about how to bring things out of chaos and pull them together to work smoothly to work through a major disaster. I am almost sad to leave here.

Leader Reflection

- What stands out for you in this narrative regarding resilience?
- What elements of this narrative link to the aspects of resilience you are working with?
- What other elements of the narrative are important to you, and why?

5

Hurricane Katrina—a Police Officer's Experience: Analysis

Wendy's narrative describes how she survived during her deployment over several weeks in the Hurricane Katrina disaster area in New Orleans, Louisiana, and demonstrates huge levels of resilience and the ability to move beyond the horror she encountered in such a disaster area. It illustrates some remarkable points with regard to resilience. Although leaders may never find themselves serving in such a disaster area, we believe there are many valuable lessons we can learn from Wendy's narrative.

Self-reflection

Wendy says she uses journaling as a form of spiritual practice and believes that journaling during the situation described in her narrative allowed her time to self-reflect on her day-to-day activities, centre herself, and prepare for the following days. She manages her emotions and feelings on paper rather than burying or denying them.

Current research in the police community (Smith and Charles 2010; Charles 2009) is finding that one of the primary ways officers attend to the high level of emotions is through self-reflection. It is very significant that Wendy identifies this journaling as a spiritual practice. Sometimes this type of spiritual practice can be more accessible and acceptable to people because it has less negative connotations than prayer or meditation.

Wendy's reflections are deep and thought-provoking as she explores existential questions of what it means to be human in the midst of disaster. What does it mean to serve when the environment is so dangerous and those you serve act in ways that are atypical of those in need? How does this form of spiritual practice assist one in staying centred and focused through the crisis?

As one police officer in Charles' research says: "What I love most about police work is seeing humanity at its core. I don't consider any of that to be challenging. I consider all of that to be a gift. You can meet each person right where he or she is" (Charles 2005: 110).

As you explore Wendy's words and thoughts in the narrative, consider how you respond in situations so contrary to what you know. What can you hold onto in complete crises? More than just coping yourself, how can you help not only yourself, but also others out of the midst of chaos into growth and understanding?

Wendy's words express a certain level of excitement as she prepares to leave her position as a full-time police officer and respond to the devastation in New Orleans. She has trained for years to respond to such disasters and is prepared to exhibit her strengths and training. Police officers are dedicated to training, and the organization commits a huge amount of resources to the various aspects of training police officers because they may well make the difference between life and death in a police officer's preparation for a variety of threats. Much of that training involves self-analysis or reflection regarding strengths and weaknesses, and engaging in training to enhance skills. We feel this emphasis placed on training is one of the key reasons why the police and police organization are so resilient and capable of building resilience.

Certainly, we can correlate the importance of training in any leadership position. Leaders in any context prepare themselves for the challenges within their environment. This type of preparation is imperative to maintain resilience. In addition to training, police officers depend on the experiences from the job to learn and grow. This also may be beneficial to leaders who, faced with crises, reflect on training and experience to enhance their abilities to survive and thrive beyond an individual crisis. Wendy's use of self-reflection is an excellent example of preparing, training, and moving into growth from crises.

Wendy states in the narrative that she writes in her journal every night or end of shift. She finds comfort in placing the events of the day on paper, thereby removing them from her thoughts. It is interesting to see how effective this appears to be for her when considering the extremely long hours, dangerous environments, and high demands she has to contend with. She still finds the time to write, to note, what is important to her, to comfort herself. This is very powerful, and rather undermines the common reason people give for not using self-reflective journals – that they lack the time to write them.

Reflective practice seems a key element to building resilience, and in all the narratives in this text you will see evidence of people reflecting in a variety of ways. As a result, we shall explore it further in the next section. It is a topic we return to in Chapter 7.

Reflective Practice

Schön (1983) identifies two forms of reflection: reflecting *in* action, which is reflecting while we are engaged in the action, and reflecting *on* action, where we look back on the action and event and consider how it went, what went well, and what could have been done differently or developed further. We see both of these forms of reflection in the narratives. A great deal has been written about reflective practice, how to do it, and its benefits, and it is not within our remit to cover this in detail here. Reflective practice is a skill that develops the more you practise it, though, and there are many resources available to assist you in developing this skill. It does take time, discipline, and energy, but it is a flexible, free, and powerful tool that you may wish to have in your armoury for the development of greater resilience.

Experiential Learning

Reflection is a powerful tool, but ideally you need some form of structure for the reflection process, otherwise you can go on and on reflecting on the event and never really get anywhere. We find in our teaching that a useful structure to assist in guiding reflections is the Experiential Learning Cycle (ELC) developed by David Kolb (1983). Kolb argues that we do not fully capitalize on the learning that we can draw from a situation or experience unless we go completely around this learning cycle. A simplification of the ELC that we have worked with and find easy to use is shown in Figure 5.1.

In Figure 5.1, the "Experience" is the action you are reflecting upon. The "What?" aspect covers what happened, what you felt and thought at the time. You then move on to the "So What?" stage to consider what this means, why that might have happened, and what the consequences and implications are. The "Now What?" stage moves you to the action planning – what are you going to do now, what is your next step? You then implement those ideas, and the cycle begins again.

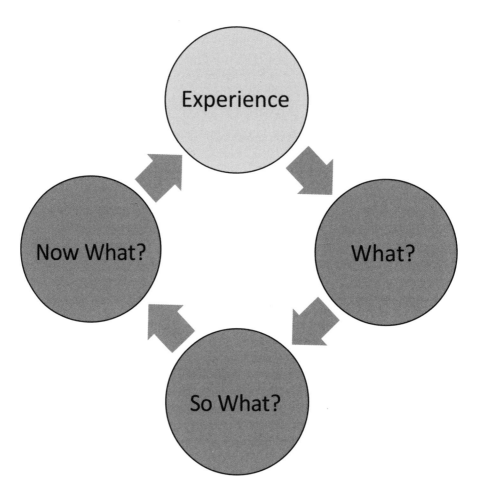

Figure 5.1   **Adaptation of Kolb's Experiential Learning Cycle**

We find that people are generally good at reflecting on one or two aspects of this cycle, but often get stuck at some point, for example at the "What?" stage. They can then go over and over the same things, worrying, hoping perhaps that if they think about what happened, the next time things will be different. Hence the benefit of the ELC in encouraging you not to dwell for too long on any particular stage, but to move on to the next stage and ensure you move completely around the learning cycle.

Would you find it useful to use this learning cycle in your reflections on the questions we have asked in this book? How might this help you?

Sense of Calling

From Wendy's description of "answering an ad" as the beginning of her career, it does not appear that she saw entering the police as a calling. However, she says later in her narrative that she recognizes that her interest in death investigations now gives her meaning and purpose for why she is in the police profession. She says her purpose is "to give the dead the last bit of dignity I could as they left this world". Her dedication to this type of investigation is extraordinary.

She also demonstrates a higher sense of calling by adding other duties to her police career. Wendy's participation in DMORT with FEMA (Federal Emergency Management Agency) is an added responsibility, requiring extensive training and time commitment.

We explore this question of calling further in Chapter 7.

Over-commitment

Often leaders task themselves with additional jobs, responsibilities, and burdens. One concern about this dedication to service in any organization or community which is connected to our exploration of resilience is the risk of over-commitment and burnout. Research has shown that many police officers become so enthralled in their work that they lose themselves, finding more and more to do as they search for things that lift them, that bring them to their highest selves (Fontana 2003). As an example, one police officer in Charles' research said: "My wife always felt like the victims and the defendant moved into her house with me, because I allow the investigation to intrude to every fiber of my body. You really want to provide a quality service to the victims because what they've gone through is horrendous" (Charles 2005: 112).

This over-commitment can lead to compassion fatigue, which Figley (1999) suggests results from a deep level of caring about a profession from the person, but a lack of appreciation from those surrounding them in their profession about the issues and what is really involved.

This type of fatigue (Police Compassion Fatigue, or PCF) is most often seen in those who deal with trauma. The symptoms of compassion fatigue can, however, be experienced by all leaders. Our relationship with trauma may not be as frequent as those on the front line of policing. However, our family history, personal lives, or work environment may provide plenty of opportunities to experience the effects of compassion fatigue.

Table 5.1 provides us with a few examples of compassion fatigue and its pervasiveness in every area of an individual's life. Leaders can learn from this tendency of over-commitment, and addressing this is clearly an important element in building resilience. It is a heavy responsibility for any leader to remain self-aware of their limitations and balance effectively their personal and professional lives. In addition, as a leader, you may recognize employees or fellow workers who over-extend themselves to the point of exhaustion or illness. So when do you say "enough"? Certainly, we can acknowledge where we are as leaders and remain aware of what our employees are doing. We can also self-reflect, and perhaps journal our thoughts.

Table 5.1   Examples of some effects of compassion fatigue

Cognitive	Emotional	Behavioural	Spiritual	Personal Relations
Decrease in concentration	Anger	Impatient	Loss of purpose	Withdrawal
Apathy	Depression	Moody	Pervasive hopelessness	Loneliness
Rigidity	Fear	Sleep disturbance	Loss of faith	Projection of anger

Source: Summarized from Figley (1999: 41).

Preparation and Training

Wendy has accumulated many hours of training in order to prepare her for deployment. However, her description of the stifling weather, the sheer devastation of the city, the horror of working with so many dead bodies, and the fear is beyond anything known to her. As leaders, we need to prepare and train for our responsibilities in our workplace. Our abilities to engage in training create plasticity within our brains (Begley 2007). We become more flexible, building more choice in the process. Leadership training should emphasize training that stretches us beyond our limits. For if we can break outside our comfort zone, we open up to creativity and strength when examining "what's next".

One of the most valuable techniques we can learn and teach ourselves and our employees is problem-solving. By using critical thinking skills and training to explore all options in the problem as well as all resources available, we create the ability to think beyond the problem and offer choices to solve the issue in front of us. When our environment becomes unfamiliar, it may be imperative to identify what the primary issues are and to think creatively and beyond the boundaries of what is most familiar.

Do you take full advantage of the training opportunities that are open to you? Do you feel you have access to sufficient training opportunities to enable you to cope with the challenges you have to deal with? If not, what might you be able to do about that?

As leaders, our acceptance of our environment may be crucial to moving beyond a crisis and developing our resilience. Wendy arrives in New Orleans to find herself in buildings without water or air conditioning. The heat and humidity are stifling, yet she finds herself processing her situation and making conscious choices to move beyond her conditions. This goes against Maslow's argument and his hierarchy that we explored in Chapter 3. In this theory, Maslow (1968) asserts that there is within human beings a need for growth, and based on this drive, he suggests that people are motivated by needs, ordered in the hierarchy discussed in Chapter 3. Maslow argues that the lower needs in the hierarchy have to be satisfied first, and once these have been met, a person's motivation moves to the next level, and ultimately to their self-actualization needs. Guirdham (1995: 35) questions this concept of a hierarchy of needs, and argues that the idea that needs at different levels cannot simultaneously motivate behaviour has been widely challenged. Tennant (1993: 14) also argues that it is "patently untrue that one must attend to the lower levels before the higher". Wendy is clearly operating at the self-actualized level, whilst her base-level physiological needs are not being met. She has created flexibility in her abilities to accept where she is, and thereby respond with recognition that the situation or crisis is not permanent. She is able to remain hopeful. Certainly, emotions run high during crises. As leaders, our recognition of how we are feeling is critical to our flexibility to adapt to our environment.

Wendy also describes "organized chaos" in her environment. Her preparation and training give her a basic concept where she may know what a disaster scene should look like, but she also needs the flexibility to expand beyond that picture and accept the chaos. Can you move beyond your comfort area to look at other ways to respond to the difficult situations you experience?

When the environment surrounding you is difficult, if not dangerous, why might it be important for you to develop this ability, and how could you develop it? Can you remain clear and conscious about your choices and how you may respond?

Resilience in the Midst of Danger

Wendy describes being very uncomfortable when trying to help pick up the bodies in the disaster area while being surrounded by gunfire. She is trying to be of service in a community, but clearly identifies how vulnerable she feels without her gun and bulletproof vest. She writes of how confusing it is when working to try to help, yet at the same time seeing gangs overrunning the city and placing the teams' lives in danger.

In the narrative, Wendy says she says feels vulnerable without her gun and vest. We find this very interesting. Does this mean that she does not feel vulnerable when she has these? This is interesting, since a gun and vest can only ever provide fairly limited protection. Do the gun and vest help with Wendy's resilience? Do leaders have things they carry, wear, or think of that help with their resilience? What about a suit, nice shoes, carrying a folder or book? Are these things providing resilience in the mind or physically?

Leaders may often be confronted with conflicting information or environments. Employees may act contrary to the help we attempt to provide them. Some may act violently when we have to deliver financially bad information or announce downsizing or organizational closures. Fontana (2003) identifies that this can be hugely emotionally draining for leaders who finds their work meaningful and purposeful. How can we maintain our vision and moral compass during these stressful times? Do you have support systems in place to assist during these stressful encounters?

Wendy's journal details the incredibly long hours she worked and how she managed to cope, even during 36-hour days. She finds moments where she can grab some sleep, but similar to an intern working long hours in a hospital, she generally just carries on.

She also describes working in extreme heat wearing a Tyvek suit, yet she seems somehow to remain resilient and manage her stress levels. Her attitude and stress seem to be manageable. How does she cope with the stress and her changing environment?

We argue that one of the most powerful management tools she utilizes is to remember that she is doing this in service of others. She has created meaning and purpose within her life, and is being guided by this. Wendy's identification of finding meaning and purpose in her work parallels the work of Victor Frankl (1984). Through the horror of death, isolation, and human suffering, Wendy acknowledges that there is purpose for her to be there and to "help" in whatever way she can. Frankl's work *Man's Search for Meaning* (1984) is about the story of his survival of Nazi concentration camps. His experiences left him with the conclusion that "Life ultimately means taking the responsibility to find the right answer to its problems and to fulfill the tasks which it constantly sets for each individual" (Frankl 1984: 97). He also asserts that the search for a sense of meaning is the primary motivational force in people's lives (Frankl 1984: 121), and reports a survey undertaken in the USA that found that 78 per cent of the 7,948 college students surveyed said that their first goal was finding a meaning and purpose to their life (Frankl 1984: 122). In the second half of *Man's Search for Meaning*, Frankl introduces his school of thought with regard to logotherapy. The term "logotherapy" is derived from *logos*, the Greek word for "meaning". Frankl believes that the most effective therapy for many people is to discover the purpose of their lives. Frankl believes that the origins of so many self-destructive patterns and behaviours lies in people's existential frustration – their inability to see meaning in their lives.

In the narrative, Wendy describes the entire team spending a few minutes of silence together each morning to remember the victims. This type of sharing again offers hope in times when we can get stuck in asking ourselves why this had to happen. The DMORT members share these moments together, thereby creating a community of common thought surrounding their purpose.

In another passage, Wendy shares a very disturbing scene of a hospital where she and her team have located several dead patients still attached to machines designed to keep them alive. The machines and instruments continue to function while the patients have long since passed. Wendy questions the reasons why they were left behind and whether they were aware of their situation prior to dying. Wendy describes a child tied to a fence and a man tied to a tree. She questions why the little girl was alone.

Certainly, the existential questioning that Wendy is experiencing can lead an individual to become cynical and fatigued. In fact, Wendy openly writes of feeling bothered by the scenes before her in the disaster area. According to Chopra (2010), one of the differences in individuals who are happy compared to those who are unhappy is that the happy people are exercising voluntary choices over how they live. Wendy, we argue, is able to cope with these difficulties partly because she remembers her voluntary choice to go to New Orleans and offer her services.

When we can also accept difficult situations like those experienced by Wendy in New Orleans as being beyond our knowing and surrender to the subtle sense of flow and mystery, we are better able to cope. In recent research within the police community conducted by Charles (2009), there is a sense of knowing that man's justice is often ineffective. Police officers interviewed described their belief that beyond man's justice there is a "higher form of justice". While a particular scene may be beyond comprehension, there is faith that there is another realm of understanding.

As leaders, we are often looked upon to have each and every answer for everyone. It is ridiculous to think that we can provide all the answers, and if we set out to try and meet this need, we are setting ourselves up for immediate failure. Often it may serve us, as leaders, to acknowledge our limitations and surrender to the flow and mystery. When we can move into a sense of flow in our circumstances, we open ourselves to the mystery.

Some of that mystery may come from seeing that which has no reference. Wendy shares the sheer number of bodies that they must process, identify, and prepare for burial. She describes seeing a dead person with a television remote control attached to his waist; another with a life jacket on; bodies that had already been previously prepared for burial before the floods, and which must now be re-prepared again. The scenes are unbelievable. There are no words that provide adequate explanation, but they demonstrate how much humans can endure and how resilient they can be.

Leaders may find themselves in situations where their reality does not seem to fit with what they are now witnessing. While it may not be a disaster area or they may not be in danger, there are many situations where leaders may be called to respond to the "impossible". If we can surrender to the mystery, collect ourselves, and think creatively beyond our situations, we move through the impossible.

Growth and Conclusion

Wendy acknowledges her surprise that she has worked in impossible conditions for three weeks with a fantastic team of people. Wendy is not superhuman, she is a just a human being, but she has coped with a quite extraordinary situation using some extraordinary skills and strategies. With training, effort, and application, these skills and strategies can be developed by others – including you. More than surviving, though, Wendy recognizes the strengths, skills, and knowledge she has acquired through this crisis. Through Wendy's choice to look at the crisis as a moment in time in which to learn and grow, she has accomplished just that. She has creatively thought through very tragic circumstances and found the resilience to thrive beyond the crisis. By surrendering to the flow and mystery of life, regardless of the situation, she has found a community of others who choose to serve with the highest levels of service and compassion.

Wendy worked tirelessly in service and in the background in New Orleans – an unsung hero. How much we all owe to Wendy and other people like her. How many people in your own organizations and communities are unsung heroes, working tirelessly in the background? Is there anything you can do to show these people that you recognize and appreciate their efforts? What might be the effect on them and their resilience if you did this? What might be the affect on your own resilience?

Wendy's humility shows in her descriptions of having learned so much and knowing that she helped by working in the background, doing work that many could not or would not do. As leaders, Wendy's narrative can provide an excellent opportunity to see what we can do in the heat of crisis if we just put our minds to it. When we can voluntarily choose to view our circumstances as momentary in life, we can create space for the most miraculous work to occur. This is how powerful these choices of living and conditions of life can be for us. As leaders, we are obligated to take the challenge for ourselves and lead by example. Perhaps we can provide that same growth to those who rely on us for their learning.

Case 3

6

Assistance Required – Can You Respond?

Andrew. A. Malcolm

Introduction

The incident I describe relates to a personal journey that followed my response to a call for assistance from fellow officers. It describes the incident that immediately followed, the outcomes of answering that call, the injury I received, and the outcomes of this injury in the line of duty. In the end, this injury ended my police career and caused me to completely re-evaluate my life.

There is nothing overly remarkable in the story; countless other police officers have experienced similar incidents, though fewer have had their careers cut short by such events. How my life developed as a result is different, and by any standard quite unusual. As I tell the story, I am conscious of a common thread running through it – that thread is my Christian faith. It is this faith, my spirituality, which eventually led me to explore and subsequently enter another vocation – a vocation in which I am completely fulfilled.

The Beginning

My first vocation, as far as work was concerned, was the police. I grew up in the late 1950s, early 1960s, the product of parents who were loving and supportive of me in all I did, and definitely wanting "better" for me than they had. My father and mother were born in the early part of the twentieth century and witnessed the First World War, the Depression and the Second World War; certainly, fighting in the Second World War had a great impact on my father. Both he and my mother worked hard to provide all they could for me. They had little money, but there was no doubt they were absolutely determined I would have more than they. I had it drummed into me to get a job with "prospects" – something fulfilling, but one that would be a job for life.

I toyed with the idea of teaching, but my early ventures into academia were unsuccessful! I thought of the Army, and wanted to follow my father and become an officer. That avenue was ruled out, though, as a result of my disastrous GCE (General Certificate of Education) results. I thought of joining my father's old regiment as a regular soldier, and made a number of enquiries into this. However, at the time of doing this I came across an advert asking for young men and women to join the Police Cadets, I applied, was accepted, and left home for the first time for an adventure and what was for me, I hoped, a life-long career. Almost two years later I transferred to another force and was appointed as a constable in May 1974. From there, over the years, my career developed with work in operational policing, traffic, community policing, and criminal investigation work. I was promoted to sergeant and again worked in an operational environment, eventually leading to my post as sergeant in charge of a specialist unit. This was a team which dealt with all incidents of major public disorder and searches of serious crime scenes in my force area. The training and the work were rigorous and demanding, but I loved it. We were at the heart of all major incidents throughout the force area and beyond. It was a role I relished, and I felt like I'd been waiting all my working life for such a post. What follows is what happened on a typical shift on the unit … this night was to be very different, though.

The Call for Assistance

It had been a hot summer day which had turned into a very warm and pleasant evening as my colleagues and I reported for night duty. I was a sergeant in charge of 10 officers on what was called the Support Unit. Our prime responsibility on this specialist squad was to act as a highly mobile team of officers who were called upon to search major crime scenes, target crime hot-spots, but primarily to deal with acts of disorder ranging from riots to demonstrations and general street disturbances. This was work I was made for. I had been an operational police officer for nearly twenty years, working in a variety of operational roles, relishing the opportunity to make a difference. In fact, whilst this is a cliché, the ability to make a difference and serve others was the reason I first joined the police, and is part of that common thread running through my story. It was, as I was to later find out, a feeling that I would now describe as spiritual, in the sense that something from within my soul attracted me to work that had a service element to it.

This particular night, which was to become life-changing for me, was like many other night shifts – hot, many people had begun their annual summer holidays, and the pubs and clubs were full. With the inevitable quantities of alcohol that would be consumed, trouble would be a key feature of the night's policing across the county area in which I operated. Although a little apprehensive, I was not worried or concerned as it was work as normal, and in fact there was a sense of excitement and apprehension about what the night would bring. We were ready for it "to kick off".

Things turned out as predicted. A number of disturbances in and around public houses as well as a flurry of street skirmishes and brawls in the first few hours of the shift were all dealt with swiftly. A number of arrests for drunkenness as well as public order offences laid the way for the rest of the evening to continue in the same manner. The numbers of people going into the local night clubs reinforced this, and we expected a busy night in the large industrial town in which we were centred. Just after 1 a.m. we went into the local police station to deposit another batch of miscreants and snatch what we could in terms of food and drink before "kicking-out" time at 2 a.m. Being in charge of the unit, I had a county-wide role, so liaised regularly with our headquarters, which monitored what was taking place across the force area and looked to deploy us wherever the need arose. I responded to one of these calls, where an inspector from a town some 25 miles away from where we were was requesting assistance with a large-scale disturbance they were dealing with. As this town was smaller than the one we were in, fewer officers were available to deal with such an incident. I was told things were getting out of hand. Any call for assistance from a fellow officer is always treated with the utmost urgency, and I immediately gathered my men and we travelled at speed to the place where we were needed.

On arrival at the town, we were directed to one particular public house around which large numbers of people were stood outside and in the general area. The atmosphere was volatile, and apparently numerous skirmishes had broken out prior to our arrival, the remnants of which were still bubbling. People were shouting and swearing, some were being held back by their friends from fighting. Some elements within the troublemakers identified the increase in police presence and began turning their abuse towards my officers. We were an extremely experienced team in public disorder issues, and the possibilities of further and more serious trouble were very real. The situation was very tense, and my experience told me that if the crowds were not dispersed quickly, then undoubtedly further trouble would continue, with the likelihood of things getting far more out of hand and the potential for serious injury amongst those on the streets.

What followed took the usual form: individuals were told to leave the scene and stop swearing. Many responded to this request, but some did not, and as a result some arrests followed. After some time we successfully quelled this large disturbance and managed to get the vast majority of people away from the scene. They went on their way in the flotilla of taxis that always seems to appear on these occasions. The late-night restaurants would have a bumper trade now, and no doubt the local police would be kept busy for the rest of the night with the subsequent domestic disputes that would arise as the revellers arrived home. There were, however, a small minority who decided to descend on the nearby police station to remonstrate about the arrest of some of their friends. I went with my team to deal with this, and as our Support Unit inspector arrested one person, one of their friends decided to attack him. I stepped in to stop this, and became involved in a violent struggle. In the course of this I arrested the man. During the struggle, this arrested man fell on me, causing me to fall backwards onto my back. Immediately I felt a severe pain in my back and right leg. Looking down, I could see my leg was hugely distorted and appeared out of joint. The pain that engulfed me was horrendous, and I felt I was about to pass out. However, I kept hold of the arrested man until my officers took him away. I was pleased I didn't "lose" my prisoner – a cardinal sin for all police officers!

The Injury and Its Ramifications

After the incident, I was taken to hospital in the police van – it seemed easier and quicker without bothering an already busy ambulance service. On arrival at the hospital, they looked at my leg; it was hugely swollen, so they bandaged it and told me to return the following day. On my return to hospital the following day, I was told my kneecap had been dislocated, I had possible damage to my cruciate ligaments, and my back was badly bruised. My leg was put in plaster for two months, and I began a course of extensive physiotherapy. Ominously, a doctor said to me that I would have been better breaking the leg as opposed to what had happened to it. He said breaks healed better. I didn't take much notice of this, feeling I would be back at work within a fortnight at most.

Some months after the incident, I was still off work; I began to entertain the possibility that what had happened was more serious than I had thought. Throughout that time, the officers I worked with were fantastic; they would often call and see me, even take me for a drink. At higher ranks, though, the support was non-existent; I thought there seemed little or no appreciation of my situation. By this time, I'd been off work for a considerable period and didn't feel I was making much progress. My knee was still very, very painful, and my physical activity was severely curtailed. My own general practitioner (GP) kept signing me off work as I was unfit to return to operational duties. Indeed, the requirement of the service was that you had to be fit enough to perform operational duties, and clearly I wasn't; I began to fear for my future. I began to harbour thoughts that I might never be able to return to the job I loved. I was under 40 years of age with two young children, and knew I would not be penniless, but the financial prospects and the thought that I might not be able to carry on with my career began to impact on me. Nobody seemed interested in this nor tried to help me find a solution to the problem.

I decided to try to do something about the situation myself, and eventually heard of a position in a department that trained newly promoted police sergeants. I decided to grasp the situation and apply, my reasoning being that as this was a non-operational post, I would be unlikely to exacerbate my injury. I did apply, and to my joy found that I was appointed, and also told I was to be promoted to the rank of inspector. This was a job I'd never done before, and I wasn't even sure I was cut out for it – but it was a chance to get back to work and develop my career. I was at the training unit for eighteen months, and during that time I underwent another operation on my knee. The feelings of dashing headlong towards a point where I couldn't perform my job began to come back. If I couldn't do *this* job without having to have time off, then how could I ever get back to an operational role?

After eighteen months in this role, I had to return to operational policing as my contract was about to expire. Some months after my return, the physical nature of my role began to once more take its toll and the physical pain became very debilitating. I had no choice but to see my GP again. The moment I saw him and explained my situation, he immediately signed me off work, saying I shouldn't do what I was doing as I was running the risk of further damaging my knee. It was at this point that I finally knew within myself my career was over. This was a horrendous blow. I had a young family and was only 40 years of age; I was devastated. I was doing a job I loved, was good at, and my future prospects were suddenly dashed.

I believe the way the organization – and by that I mean those responsible for personnel issue in the force – dealt with me at this time made a difficult situation worse. As an example, the Force Medical Officer told me that if I took double the dose of a painkiller I was prescribed, this would mask the pain sufficiently for me to return to work. Two senior police officers instructed me to comply with this direction and questioned why I wouldn't. I told them my own GP had specifically told me to take as few painkillers as possible so as not to mask the pain; doing so could cause more damage. I felt hectored, criticized, and disbelieved as to why I was off work. Frankly, I felt bitter that after almost 25 years of service and sacrifice, willingly and acceptingly, to the job and the people I served, I was written off and treated in such a manner. Some time later, after direct intervention from my own GP, I was formally told that my police career was over. There was little or no contact from then onwards with any senior member of the organization. I felt I no longer existed to them. I was angry and yet depressed at this, but still felt proud that I had been a police officer. I knew I would do something – it isn't in my nature not to. But what would I do?

My Future Direction

At the beginning of this story, I said there was a common thread running through it – a thread characterized by my Christian faith. In this very difficult period, I had to call on all the reserves I could find, including my faith, to deal with the issues that were affecting me and my family. My family were at the forefront of my mind, for practical reasons. On reflecting now on the incident, I have come to see the day I was injured as both one of the worst days of my life, because of all the repercussions that I am still experiencing to this day, and yet also one of the best. During those six months off work, I was able to spend quality time with my family and two young children as they grew up – a blessing, and because of my very busy working life as a police officer, the first time I had been able to do this in my life.

Make no mistake, there were many "dark nights of the soul", but often I found that inextricably, these had light cast on them by my faith. Looking back now, these times consisted of feeling, at best, "like a fish out of water", not able to function in an environment other than that I was used to. At worst, there were days and weeks where I was simply inert, not knowing what to do. I worked for myself, undertaking consultancy in areas of management and leadership as well as in security, but something always seemed to be missing; I couldn't find anything that really suited me.

Over time, and in small and often unnoticed ways, the spiritual rose above and quelled my mental and physical angst, albeit sometimes only temporarily – but it kept making its presence known. I came to see that prior to the injury, my life was one of doing; constantly busying myself with work. Over the months and years afterwards, I slowly began to recognize that my life had refocused into one that saw the priority in living as being; taking the time to reflect on what I did rather than just doing it. I did not blame God for the injury – rather, I saw His hand in moving me to a workplace for which I am eminently suited. What He did with me after the injury was to accompany me through all the issues that arose.

I seemed destined to enter a profession where money was not the main or motivating factor. In the early 1970s, this was certainly the case for the police service. I had joined the service in the hope of doing something useful for society and to make a difference. On reflection, I realize I was being called to serve even then. My willingness to serve and help others extended throughout my police career, and to instances such as the one I have described where I responded to a call for assistance from colleagues. The common thread is that then, as now, I have always felt God's hand in my life and decisions I have made, but have only comparatively recently begun to fully realize this. Over time, my sense of self, my sense of the spiritual, became stronger and easier for me to recognize. Gradually, I began to see that God was directing me to explore another vocation – another way to serve. Finally, some ten years after my injury, I began theological training, culminating in my ordination as a priest in the Anglican Church. I had moved from the Crook to the Cross!

Leader Reflection

- What stands out for you in this narrative regarding resilience?
- What elements of this narrative link to the aspects of resilience you are working with?
- What other elements of the narrative are important to you, and why?

7

Assistance Required – Can You Respond?: Analysis

Physical, Mental, and Spiritual Challenges

Andrew's narrative clearly highlights the physical challenges in police work and the physical injuries that can often be sustained by officers in the line of duty. That duty is in the service and protection of others – you and me – in order to make the world a safer place for us all. These physical threats and injuries are often fairly easy to recognize. This narrative, though, also clearly identifies the mental and spiritual challenges and wounds in these areas that can so often occur in both police work and leadership more generally, but which are so often under the surface and left unrecognized, unsupported, untreated, and unresolved.

If we are to develop effective resilience, then, as discussed in Chapter 1, it seems crucial that we consider all these various challenges in a holistic way, rather than focusing only on the physical because this is easier to identify and treat. We identified one holistic model in the Introduction called the Global Fitness Framework (GFF), developed by Rayment and Smith (2013). This is useful in highlighting the different aspects of fitness that we are discussing here.

Andrew's narrative draws our attention to the physical, mental, and spiritual challenges that are highlighted in the GFF at the individual level. These challenges can be extended and also considered at the organizational level ("group" in the GFF). Another holistic model which provides more details of what may be considered at the individual and organizational levels is shown in Figure 7.1.

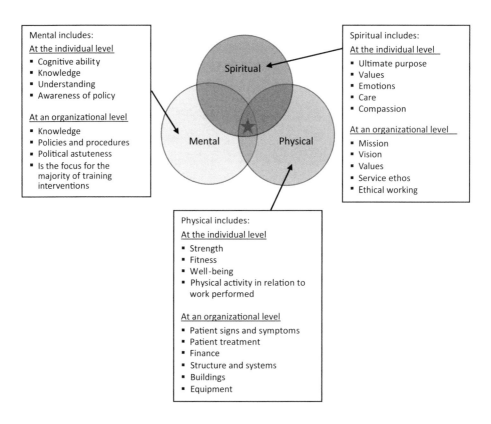

Mental includes:

At the individual level

- Cognitive ability
- Knowledge
- Understanding
- Awareness of policy

At an organizational level

- Knowledge
- Policies and procedures
- Political astuteness
- Is the focus for the majority of training interventions

Spiritual includes:

At the individual level

- Ultimate purpose
- Values
- Emotions
- Care
- Compassion

At an organizational level

- Mission
- Vision
- Values
- Service ethos
- Ethical working

Spiritual

Mental   Physical

Physical includes:

At the individual level

- Strength
- Fitness
- Well-being
- Physical activity in relation to work performed

At an organizational level

- Patient signs and symptoms
- Patient treatment
- Finance
- Structure and systems
- Buildings
- Equipment

Figure 7.1   A holistic approach to leadership

Source: Smith and Malcolm (2010: 55).

In this model, the focus is on those who work in the National Health Service (NHS) in the UK, but it applies equally to policing, or in fact any other area of work. This way of expressing a holistic approach to leadership is an adaptation of the Action Centred Leadership (ACL) model devised by John Adair (Adair and Nelson 2004: 4–5), and maintains some of the key principles emphasized in the ACL model. This may be a useful approach, as many in leadership roles will be familiar with Adair's ACL approach and the principles it emphasizes. The principles in the ACL model also apply in Figure 7.1, including the importance of balance, having an equal focus between all three areas, and the interaction between the different elements as well as the elements themselves. Many see policing and leadership as primarily physical activities, including managing resources, finance, and people, but a key argument in this text is that physical effort is neither sustainable nor effective without equal attention being paid to the other aspects highlighted in Figure 7.1 – namely, the mental and spiritual aspects of a person's and organization's makeup. This model suggests that for policing and leadership to be effective, we need to consider the physical, mental, and spiritual challenges in equal measure.

There are numerous individual physical and mental challenges identified in Andrew's narrative that are important considerations in our quest for the development of greater resilience: the sacrifices in terms of time with family and friends that are made by police officers in the long and unsocial hours they work, and at times when the majority are on holiday or celebrating. At a deeper level, these sacrifices also include spiritual components.

Another physical and mental challenge is the food and drinks being "snatched on the run". In operational policing, there are often no real meal breaks. Herrick (2011), however, argues that snatching food and drink on the run on a regular and long-term basis may not be good for long-term health. This is magnified because unhealthy food is often eaten in these situations, according to Woodham (1995: 79). Herrick suggests that eating slowly gives your system time for the digestive and hormonal processes to take place so the signals get to the hypothalamus in your brain, which then helps prevent overeating and weight gain. In workplaces generally, how many employees and leaders now work through their meal breaks in order to get the job done, and have no real break? As a leader, do you overtly or covertly encourage this?

Although not directly mentioned in the narrative, there are also the ongoing challenges relating to the resulting paperwork that will no doubt be in the back of Andrew's mind as he undertakes the work. He will be conscious of the need to justify his decisions and approach in this paperwork, and the ever-present threat of litigation claims being made is likely to be hanging over him – two of the most stressful aspects of police work, according to Alexander et al. (2011: 42).

Many of these physical, mental, and spiritual challenges of being a police officer are frequently not recognized within policing. We argue, however, that these challenges are often even less recognized within leadership roles more broadly, even though a leadership position can bring many similar demands. What is the effect of this over the long term on the leader's resilience?

Often leaders also work long, unsociable hours. With globalization, the ability to travel, and need to cope with the rapid pace of change, many leaders are travelling more and for longer for their work, and thus also have to be away from their friends and family on a regular basis. Could this be one of the reasons why divorce rates are as high as they are in the West? According to a survey by the American Psychological Association (2012), current figures suggest that 40–50 per cent of married couples in the United States get divorced. As a small example, we worked with a manager recently who had not seen his three-month-old baby at all because of the demands of his work and the need to work in a different country from his wife and child. We are left wondering what the impact from this will be on this leader, his child, wife, and relationships.

Leaders heavily influence the culture in organizations, and can easily shape a long-hours culture. One leader we knew well, for example, was regularly working 16-hour days. This might be fine for the leader if she wished to do that, but unspokenly, this was what members of her team considered was expected of them, so they were all doing the same.

If we are looking at building a greater resilience, at the end of the day, when all the discussions, techniques, and strategies for working more effectively and smartly have ended, when all the reasons for not doing have been voiced, we need to remember we are human beings and ask whether a major element of all this comes down to simply doing less work and having more leisure. Whilst people can criticize this type of observation and can claim we are simply not business-aware, are not aware of the reality in business, or are being naive, we would challenge this and suggest that some are frightened to ask these important questions precisely because of these criticisms. We still wonder whether leaders could say "no" more frequently, travel and work less, use computer-based methods of communication more, and spend time on themselves, their family, and friends more.

Do you experience a high workload, information overload, or demands for extensive travel? What other pressures are of most immediate concern for you? What are likely to be the long-term negative implications of these elements for you, your family, and your organization? Are the high workload, information overload, and need for extensive travel really necessary? What would actually happen if your organization demanded less from you and your employees? Could you demand less of yourself and others who work for you?

Whilst the benefits of the long hours worked might seem clear in the short term, what are the advantages of this type of culture in the long term, and what are the difficulties, drawbacks, and longer-term implications of this style of working? Is this sustainable? Are these pressures and long hours at work really sometimes excuses to get away or avoid thinking about difficult personal issues and situations?

The Spiritual Common Thread

A key aspect emphasized in Andrew's narrative is the common spiritual thread running through his life experience, which Andrew argues has impacted positively on his ability to cope with the challenges he has experienced in his life. This very much supports our assertion in the Introduction concerning the spiritual dimension being an important component of resilience. For Andrew, the spiritual dimension has a Christian focus, but of course, as we discussed in the Introduction, the spiritual aspect of resilience does not have to only equate to a Christian religious belief.

In the Introduction, we spoke mainly about a generic spirituality and the need for a broad spectrum of spirituality in a workplace such as the police service. This is important if we are truly embracing difference, but it is also a fairly easy point to make. There are dangers, though, in making spirituality too generic and losing specific aspects of beliefs and the cultural context of spirituality. This is important, otherwise what happens, as ongoing research by Malcolm (2010) with the police shows, is that spirituality and religion can then become nothing more than a "tick-in-the-box" exercise and simply about taking care not to discriminate. Spirituality is much bigger and more significant than what is considered in any equality and diversity debate. The challenge here, then, is how to embrace a wide variety of spiritual beliefs in an organization while at the same time recognizing, valuing, nurturing, and enabling individuals' free expression and practice of their own particular beliefs.

Some individuals' beliefs will be in conflict, and it seems essential that a mature, supportive, and open environment is established to talk about these differences and work effectively through the issues and conflicts that are raised. This is no easy undertaking, as many religious conflicts throughout the world over time are testament to. However, only by doing this in an organization can we achieve a truly diverse environment that engages an individual's full commitment to the leader and organization, rather than mere compliance. An example of an organization that has achieved this balance is the Centre for Excellence in Leadership, whose CEO, Lynne Sedgmore CBE, said when she was interviewed by Altman:

> *In the Centre for Excellence in Leadership we fostered a highly inclusive approach to spirituality and never attempted to hold an organizational definition of spirituality. Instead we recognized and respected all forms of religion and spirituality – and atheism or agnosticism. The only*

*proviso was that the dignity of others was respected and no offence
was made. We made the central tenet the development of staff to their
full potential, including their inner life, as well as their professional
development. We gave permission for dialog and inquiry into soul, and
meaning and purpose, as well as fostering high performance and job
satisfaction.*

(Altman 2010: 36)

Doing and Being

Andrew identifies that he has been better able to discern this spiritual thread
in his life relatively recently. The move from "doing" to "being", enforced by
his injury, clearly seems to have assisted with this. This greater focus on being
also seems to have helped facilitate a major transformation in Andrew's life as
he moved from one vocation to a very different one which provides meaning
in his life.

Lips-Wiersma and Morris (2011a) have developed the map of meaning
shown in Figure 7.2, and this clearly identifies the differing focuses of doing
and being, and emphasizes again the need for a balanced holistic approach.

Lips-Wiersma and Morris (2011a) claim the Holistic Development Model
makes meaning, and therefore meaningfulness and meaninglessness, more
visible, and so provides a clear structure to help us grasp and work with this
often very nebulous topic of meaning. As we identified in the Introduction and
discussed further in Wendy's narrative in Chapter 5, meaning is an important
aspect of the spiritual dimension, and seems one of the keys to the development
of greater resilience. It would seem that when we have a picture of what we are
on this planet for – what our meaning and purpose is – then this is likely to help
us focus, get our priorities right, and motivate us when things are tough or not
working out as we would wish.

As shown in Figure 7.2, there are four main aspects of the Holistic
Development Model. The first is the four pathways which Lips-Wiersma and
Morris (2011a) argue are the ways to find meaningful work: developing and
becoming self, unity with others, service to others, and expressing full potential.
Secondly, these four pathways are held in tension by apparently opposing
desires: the wish to meet the needs of the self, and the wish to meet the needs of
others; and the need for being (reflection) as well as the need for doing (action).

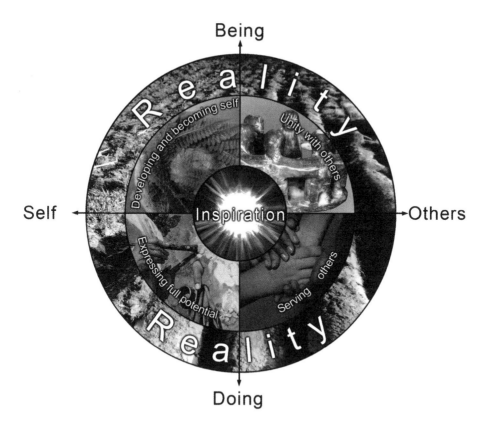

Figure 7.2   Lips-Wiersma and Morris's Holistic Development Model
Source: Lips-Wiersma and Morris (2011a).

Thirdly, all these elements are played out in the overall context of inspiration and the reality of our self and our circumstances. This reality is composed of both ideals and imperfections. We may long for the world to be a certain way, but often we experience imperfection – in ourselves or others – and how we deal with these imperfections, setbacks, and challenges of life is an important element of resilience.

This model has been further developed by Howard (2010), as shown in Figure 7.3, and she claims this model has proven particularly helpful to individuals and organizations in beginning to understand the territory of spirituality.

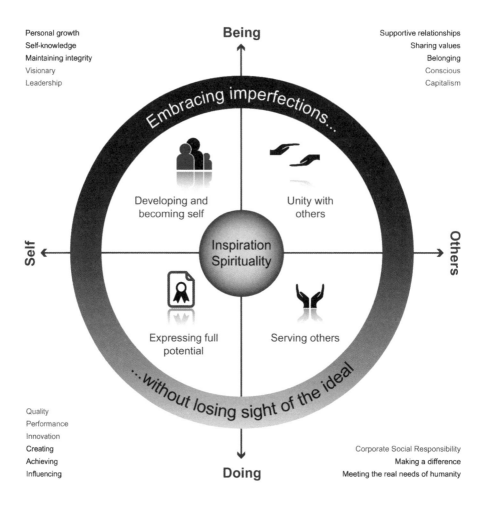

Personal growth
Self-knowledge
Maintaining integrity
Visionary
Leadership

Being

Supportive relationships
Sharing values
Belonging
Conscious
Capitalism

Embracing imperfections...

Developing and
becoming self

Unity with
others

Inspiration
Spirituality

Self

Others

Expressing full
potential

Serving others

...without losing sight of the ideal

Quality
Performance
Innovation
Creating
Achieving
Influencing

Doing

Corporate Social Responsibility
Making a difference
Meeting the real needs of humanity

Figure 7.3   Howard's adaptation of the Holistic Development Model
Source: Howard (2010).

Although Lips-Wiersma and Morris (2011a) talk about the role of the spirit as part of inspiration, Howard (2010) has added the term "spirituality" to the centre of the model, and emphasizes spirituality explicitly as being the heart of inspiration. Howard claims that this focuses attention on the central importance of spirituality as a core element of understanding who we are. She argues that from this awareness, it is then more possible to explore the various dimensions of ourselves, including who we are, what we do, and the contribution we are making to the world.

The models in Figures 7.2 and 7.3 raise a number of fundamental questions which it may be useful for you to reflect upon, for example:

- How do you know who you really are, and how do you develop more of this?

- What is the value for you of having good relationships with others? What would this bring to your life? What difficulties would it create for you? What are the things that prevent this?

- How do you express and communicate your full potential?

- What do you do for others? How do your activities influence people? What effect are you having in the world? Are these the right things for you now?

Figures 7.2 and 7.3 again emphasize the importance of achieving balance – balance between being and doing, balance between focusing on self and others. How does your life link with these four pathways? Are there some pathways that dominate? How do you achieve a balance between all four aspects? How do you think the balance impacts on building resilience?

We have found from our research with police officers that they are often largely focused on the bottom right-hand pathway in Figure 7.2 – the "serving others" quadrant. In our work as and with leaders, we find that this is a very similar focus for many leaders. Whilst there are many positive aspects to focusing on doing for others, too much focus on this area at the expense of the other three areas can be problematic. Lips-Wiersma and Morris (2011a: 86) identify a number of difficulties that can result, including martyrdom and exhaustion. "Martyrdom" is defined as any experience that causes arduous suffering, torment, and distress, and Smith and Charles (2010) have certainly found evidence of police officers experiencing this.

Figures 7.2 and 7.3 show differences of opinion as to what is at the centre of the map. Andrew's narrative clearly identifies that for him, this is a spiritual aspect. What is at the centre of this map for you? Do you have a spiritual thread running through your life? How do you know? What does this look and feel like? Are you able to take the necessary time to discern whether there is a spiritual principle guiding you, and if there is, what this might be saying to you?

Lips-Wiersma and Morris argue that the Holistic Development Model shown in Figure 7.2 helps with finding meaning. Have you thought about your purpose? What gives your life meaning? How do you know? Do you regularly re-evaluate this to see if it is the same as it was? Are your work and activities aligned with this purpose?

Sense of Calling

Linked to the above spiritual thread discussion, and the focus on meaning, a sense of calling comes across clearly in Andrew's narrative, which provides meaning to his life. Firstly, this was to be a police officer and being able to do something that made a difference, and then in a calling to join the priesthood.

It is interesting how closely priesthood and police work seem to be connected. This may be because of the link to service and ways of providing people with meaning and making a greater contribution. In this narrative, we see Andrew moving from the police to the priesthood. We have also interviewed people as part of our research who have moved the other way – priest to police officer. One officer said he always experienced conflict between being a cop or a priest. In the interview, he described "excruciating pain" in his decision to become a cop and leave the priesthood. He said he truly experienced a spiritual crisis of identity as he recognized that he was not to serve in the priesthood, but was called by God to serve as a police officer.

In Smith and Charles' (forthcoming) research with police officers, a sense of this calling to become a police officer was found to be very common, with over 90 per cent of the 30 officers interviewed identifying this. Figley (1999) and Violanti and Paton (1999) both identify that typically, police officers enter the police profession with a desire to do something meaningful, to help others, to find excitement, as well as to discover who they are.

From our experience, we do not see this sense of calling as frequently in more general leadership roles. Did you have a sense of calling to move into leadership? Leadership can been seen at different levels, from leading yourself, right through to leading a multi-billion-dollar multinational organization employing thousands of people. If you did have a sense of calling for a leadership role, was it for a particular level of leadership, or within a particular organization? If you recognize this sense of calling, has it always been the same, or has it changed? If it is not for a leadership role, then what is it for?

If it is to do something different than you are doing now, what is preventing you from responding to that call? Is the difference between your sense of calling and what you are doing now having any affect on you? If you have no sense of calling, what does this mean for you?

What does this "calling" look and feel like? How do you know you have been "called"? How do you know it is that particular role you have been called to, and that it is not simply a desire to be called?

Coping with Challenge

Andrew spoke in the narrative about his feelings during that hot evening when his injury occurred. At the start of the evening, he was looking at what was likely to be a difficult, challenging night, and for some this would have been a terrifying prospect. It is interesting, though, that in Andrew's narrative there is no mention of fear – indeed, he talks instead of excitement. Of course, absence of fear is absolutely necessary for a police officer. It would be of no use to anyone if you had 11 police officers hiding in the police station being terrified. But how is it that he can achieve this level of control over his emotions in this type of challenging, frightening situation? Is it just the type of person Andrew is, or is there more?

This is a key question in our exploration of building resilience. If a person is able to manage their emotions effectively in stressful situations and over the long term, then their resilience is going to be higher. If we can understand a little more from Andrew's narrative of how police officers do this, it may be of assistance to you in your quest for greater resilience.

As we discussed in Chapter 5, one important factor enabling Andrew to cope with the challenging situation he portrays in his narrative seems to be training. Andrew would have practised these types of public order situations and how to deal with them many times during his training. Part of this process would be the mental preparation – running over the situation many times in his mind, talking to colleagues, rehearsing what he would do when this situation arose, much like a successful athlete who rehearses the running and winning of the race many times in their mind prior to actually running.

What about you, what training have you had to cope with the stressful situations you encounter? Have you rehearsed through these types of situations in your own mind?

Andrew is also likely to have been listening, watching and learning from more senior colleagues who would have faced similar situations, either through listening to what they say, or watching them in action. Then, the gradual learning from his own experiences would come in as these were enacted over time. This building up of experience and learning is critical, and emphasizes the importance of both experiential learning and reflective practice. These are both fundamental elements of building resilience. We have touched on them already in Chapter 5, and we will return to these aspects later in this chapter.

Whilst experience is critical, there are also dangers that come with this. Andrew has to be flexible and observant because, although he may have experienced a similar situation many times before, this does not mean that this time it will be the same again. As we actually see played out in Andrew's narrative, this time was just the occasion when things were very different to the norm.

Many aspects of operational police work are very difficult to deal with. Two examples of types of situations officers encounter are given in Charles' research:

> *It was a murder of a young lady. She was shot about 19 times by her fiancée, in front of the little 5 year-old boy. There was a side of her that was askew from the norm. The little boy saw his mama shot and killed. So it went to trial and was overturned by the appeal court. Physically and emotionally, I was done.*
>
> *(Charles 2005: 127)*

> *I was a pretty young officer going out on a domestic on Christmas day. The guy had gone to the house on Christmas day when she [the victim] was away at her mother's house with the kids. They had little kids. He just destroyed the inside of this house. He painted "BITCH" on the wall, cut up the couch, destroyed the presents, and attacked the tree. She came home with these kids, they were obviously freaked out, and you just knew how much hate had to be in him to do that. It was just horrible and I'll never forget it.*
>
> *(Charles 2005: 120)*

How are police officers able to build sufficient levels of resilience to cope with having to deal with these types of situations, and what can leaders learn from them?

One factor in relation to coping with the challenge of policing is the police officers' coping strategy that Smith (2005: 247) calls "the suit of armour". Smith argues that officers can distance themselves from their feelings and emotions in order to cope with the job, rather like putting on a metaphorical suit of armour to prevent any issue penetrating their feelings, and so preventing them from feeling hurt, upset, or vulnerable. Some officers in Smith's research talked of the police uniform rather like a suit of armour, and they said putting it on made them feel more than their civilian selves (Smith 2005: 247). Many of the officers interviewed said they coped by adopting a thought process of invincibility where they could not get hurt or injured, otherwise they said they thought they would not be able to enter dangerous situations or confront dangerous criminals. As an example, one respondent in Smith's research:

> *spoke of the role he had to play ... and to do his job he had to adopt this persona that he was invincible and couldn't die otherwise he would never go into a building to confront a criminal .... He spoke of an accident he had had ... and this had really made his job difficult as he was now coming to realise that he wasn't invincible.*
>
> *(Smith 2005: 246)*

Some respondents in Smith's research shared concerns about showing any vulnerability as a police officer, which they felt would be exploited. In one example: "He said that on the street it was dangerous to show any weaknesses otherwise people would pick on that. He said public order situations, and being in a line facing a crowd of rioters was a good example – they always focused on the weaker ones" (Smith 2005: 239).

However, Smith suggests that whilst this distancing from emotions may be helpful in terms of being able to cope in the short term, it can mean that over time, officers lose touch with their feelings and emotions, as they find that the suit of armour tends to be removed less and less at the end of the shift as time goes on. This is understandable when you remember that an officer is never really off duty. They are always vulnerable to attack, always required to protect and serve.

Goffman speaks of the pressures people are often under to give a performance (Goffman 1987: 26). Police officers are likely to come under this pressure from a public expectation for them to behave in a certain way, particularly when dealing with threatening and traumatic situations and accidents. The police service may also feel the need to portray a certain image to the public, which is also likely to place demands on operational officers to act in "acceptable" ways. Czander cited Menzies as saying that employees developed "socially structured defence mechanisms" as a result of the anxiety associated with work (Czander 1993: 109). These social defences are developed over time from collective interaction, and as a result a type of unconscious agreement amongst the organization's members develops. Menzies argues that the precondition for the development of a social defence is the collective experience of anxiety; one member then articulates a way that can be used by everyone to reduce the experience of anxiety that is then accepted by the group. This is certainly evident in the police environment. Czander identified Menzies' case analysis of nurses where nurses consciously agree to engage in the behaviour associated with the defence of depersonalization (Czander 1993: 110). This is similar to that identified by Becker (cited in Moustakas 1994: 19) and Gregory (1996: 238), who note the withholding of self as a strategy used by nurses for managing personal vulnerability, and Gregory (1996: 201) talks of a "professional shield" that she observes nurses using.

The ability to distance oneself from one's feelings and emotions in challenging situations seems to be a highly desirable one that enables police officers to perform very effectively in stressful and threatening situations. This way of coping does not only apply to police officers, of course – soldiers, firefighters, surgeons, doctors, nurses, footballers, athletes, teachers, and leaders also need to do this.

Distancing oneself from one's emotions is only part of the process, however, and to be effective, the person needs to re-connect with these emotions at an appropriate time after the stressful incident, and deal with the emotions that the situation can naturally generate. This is a big part of Emotional Intelligence, and many research studies have identified the benefits of this, including Goleman (2005). It is not our intention to explore Emotional Intelligence further, as a great deal of excellent work has been done in this area. The main elements of Emotional Intelligence are awareness of both your own and others' emotions, and learning how to manage these effectively; these elements are key aspects of the development of resilience.

In policing, as we see portrayed in Andrew's narrative, and in leadership more generally, stressful situations can be almost constant for long periods. In these types of stressful work environments there can be little opportunity for discharging the physiological effects of the trauma from the body, or time for people to re-connect with and explore their emotions. The following quotation from Smith's research is an example of this:

> *I just think erm … as police officers dealing with erm, on the streets, dealing with different jobs, you tend to see and deal with it, what jobs you are giving me. It's very fast and task orientated, particularly nowadays … you haven't got much time to think about anything … you're constantly thinking all the time of what the next task is, your controllers on you, they are saying to you "OK can you go to this job, OK and on the way to that job can you stop off here."*
>
> (Smith 2005: 251)

Here, quite clearly, the police officer simply has to move on to the next job, rather than having the opportunity to process the effects of their experiences. A further example, this time from the researcher's journal, shows again this need to remove oneself from the trauma at hand:

> *[Name] shared that often he has gone to domestics and has pretended to be empathic when he hadn't been. He said that he had often made his mind up what he was going to do before he had even arrived at the home and hadn't really listened to what the people were saying. [Name] shared some similar examples in his experiences in road traffic policing. He said it was much easier that way and there was no confusion of what to do. [Name] said that he felt he had often policed situations where he had put on an act and portrayed the image that he was not affected by the horrific situation he faced, even though he went home afterwards and felt upset by it ….*
>
> (Smith 2005: 257)

It may also be, as Smith (2005: 239) identifies, that the organizational culture is such that this re-connection is seen as weak or a waste of time. Rees and Smith (2008) further examine these traumatic aspects of policing in relation to trauma theory. They discuss how trauma sufferers need to disassociate from their feelings in order not to experience "overwhelm" at the event. They also show, however, that if this is not discharged after the event, then people become habitually distanced from their emotions, and do not have the full range of emotional breadth and depth. As Bloom writes:

> *People who do not experience pain repeatedly injure themselves. People who are unable to feel anger repeatedly are victimized, whilst those*

who are chronically angry may victimize others. People who cannot feel love, compassion or tenderness have severely impaired relationships with others in their social group. People who do not experience fear lack the capacity to protect themselves.

(Bloom 1997: 39)

Constantly facing the pressures of operational policing, over time police officers can become permanently disconnected from their emotions, as found by Smith (2005). The difficulty, then, in the police work context is that officers can be seen as cold, robotic, and in their work may not be able to convey or feel any empathy for the victims of crime, or those injured in accidents. Morally, though, there are bigger questions these issues raise for the police organization, as in their home life these police officers may feel unable to connect emotionally with the partners, children, family, and friends. This may be one of the reasons for the high rates of domestic violence and high divorce rates that are seen in the police community (as identified by Smith and Charles 2010: 321).

This also raises many questions about emotions in the leadership role more generally. What is the situation with respect to dealing with people's emotions effectively in the organization you work in? Is the culture supportive of talking about how you feel, and of developing effective Emotional Intelligence?

Do you think there are times when leaders need to put their own feelings and emotions to one side to deal with difficult situations? Are you sometimes required to give a "performance"? What about situations such as redundancies, where the leader knows employees well and knows that the loss of a job will have devastating consequences for the employee and their family, and yet has no choice but to make them redundant? What about disciplinary situations, poor performance interventions, or having to close an organization completely?

If leaders do disconnect with their feelings in order to be able to deal effectively with those challenging situations they experience, how do they re-connect with their feelings again afterwards? Are they trained effectively in this area and supported and encouraged to do this, or are leaders in your organization so busy that they do not have the time to do this re-connecting?

Within the police environment, there are many support mechanisms and training interventions that are provided in order to support officers – counsellors, Trauma Risk Incident Management (TRIM), critical incident debriefers, post-traumatic stress training, to name but a few. Our experience of working in leadership more generally, however, suggests that this level of training and support is not available for leaders in many organizations. Is this type of support available in your organization? How do you cope, and how do you manage these stressful leadership duties you encounter effectively so that you ensure that you are, and remain, fully fit over the long term?

Unquestioning Response

The narrative shows that Andrew responds unquestioningly when a fellow officer calls for assistance. This clearly demonstrates the peer support so essential in the policing environment. Without this unquestioning response, the police could not work effectively and officers could be left in very vulnerable situations.

But is there a darker side to this aspect of support? Firstly, does the police organization rely too much on officer loyalty to fellow officers and operate with fewer numbers than is effective in order to save money? Is it really effective, for example in Andrew's case, for a group of 11 officers to drive 25 miles to respond to a colleague's call for assistance? Even though they went "at speed", this was still likely to have taken approximately 30 minutes before they could get to the scene, and whilst they were travelling there and back and dealing with the incident there, would this be leaving colleagues in the larger town short-staffed and vulnerable?

What about leaders more generally? Are there times when leaders can rely too much on or expect excessive loyalty from their employees? Do you expect or rely on more loyalty from your employees than is realistic? Do you rely on this loyalty more from some of your employees than others? If so, who are they and why do you do this? What are the benefits of doing this, and what may be the long-term negative consequences for you, the employees, and their resilience? Sometimes, of course, we recognize that it may be necessary, but how do you ensure that you achieve an appropriate balance in respect to this loyalty?

Andrew argues that this would never occur in reality, but we wonder whether this peer support in policing could also have a darker side and easily turn from support into being used as a powerful form of peer pressure. Could the dependency on fellow police officers to respond urgently to a call for assistance be used by peers against officers who do not toe the party line, do not turn a blind eye, or who challenge inappropriate behaviour, so that fellow police officers were all "busy" when you were in trouble and called for urgent assistance? Even if this would not actually occur in practice, is just the threat of it sufficient to keep colleagues in line?

Peer pressure does seem to be a significant aspect of the police culture, and it is identified in a number of research projects. This is not the only negative aspect that has been identified concerning the police culture, and although we have to be careful with talk of "a police culture" as this undoubtedly makes the culture appear more monolithic than it actually is, there are some common aspects to this police culture that are frequently highlighted in research. Holdaway, for example, mentions peer pressure, cynicism, and resistance to change as important elements to this police culture (Holdaway 1989: 58). Walker highlights an action-orientation, a machismo-centred self-image, and generic suspiciousness (Walker 1994: 36). The reasons for this culture have also been explored extensively. As an example, Bennet argues that the police culture is a result of a wide range of factors associated with the nature of policing, including the threat of physical danger, hostility from the public, unreasonable demands, conflicting expectations, and the pressures faced each day to get the job done (Bennet 1994: 124). Walker feels the nature of operational police work, with its danger and uncertainty, tends to bind officers to their immediate work group (Walker 1994: 36). He argues that the insularity and defensive solidarity of the groups that results amplifies a number of other cultural characteristics that emerge from the demands of operational police work.

If the above are aspects of the police culture, and the reasons for this culture are true, what impact do you think this has on police officers' and on the police organization's resilience? Do you think the police culture assists or hampers the effective development of resilience?

What about leadership more generally? Do the organization and its culture that you work within assist or restrict your ability to build resilience? Why and how specifically does it do that? What about peer pressure – do you experience peer pressure to act in a particular way? Do colleagues and managers expect a leader's loyalty to such an extent that leaders do not feel able to challenge inappropriate or unethical practices of colleagues and managers? Will there be significant personal consequences if leaders do challenge – for example, being shunned, not being supported by colleagues, losing their jobs, not being promoted, not being invited to work on important assignments or projects? If so, what are the negative consequences of this culture of inappropriate peer pressure, and how can you resist and challenge this behaviour where you feel it is necessary to do so?

Misleadership

Rayment and Smith (2011) argue that we are currently experiencing a leadership crisis globally, and suggest that a lot of what is seen as leadership is nothing of the sort, but in fact "misleadership". They identify four different types of misleadership – Missing, Misinformed, Misguided and Machiavellian – and argue that these are widespread and endemic in every aspect of our upbringing, socialization, and education. They identify the Embedded Values Cycle shown in Figure 7.4 as showing how our upbringing can influence our thoughts, attitudes, and behaviours.

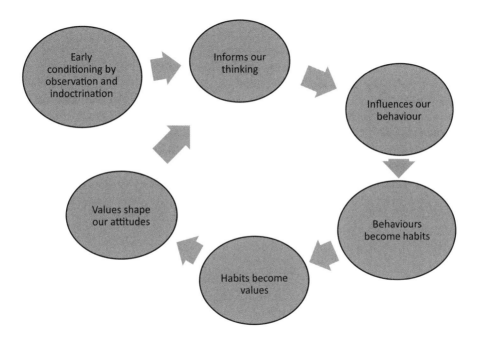

Figure 7.4   The Embedded Values Cycle
Source: Rayment and Smith (2011).

Could it be that one of the reasons why this misleadership continues and is so prevalent and frequently unchallenged is because of the peer pressure we mentioned earlier, resulting from loyalty and the expectations that fellow leaders either within or outside the organization will not challenge other leaders' inappropriate behaviours?

There are many aspects connected with the Embedded Value Cycle shown in Figure 7.4. Can you identify any others? One that links to this book's exploration is, we argue, that some of a person's resilience comes from their upbringing and early education. As an illustration of this, one author's partner and her sister have great levels of resilience, and we identify that a lot of this comes from the example set by their mother and grandmother, who were equally resilient.

We see at least one of the four forms of misleadership that Rayment and Smith (2011) identify demonstrated in the narrative – "Missing Leadership", which Rayment and Smith say is where appropriate and necessary leadership simply does not take place. We see this in the lack of support or even interest offered by the constabulary leadership to Andrew after his injury. This even goes so far as telling him to double the intake of his painkillers so he will be able to mask the pain and be able to carry on with work. We can also see the impact this has on Andrew, his feelings, motivation, and resilience.

Reflective Practice

We highlighted earlier in this chapter, and also in Chapter 5, the importance of personal reflection in the development of resilience. The Embedded Values Cycle in Figure 7.4 also emphasizes the importance of reflecting on the things that have influenced your thinking and behaviour. Are all the messages you received from your upbringing and socialization appropriate and right for the current culture, climate, and role that you are performing now? If not, which do you think are not, and what do you need to change?

Narrative's Moral

There is a very clear underlying moral coming from Andrew's narrative – perhaps "Out of crisis and difficulty comes greater good." It is a very positive and empowering moral.

Do you believe this moral applies in your own life? Do you act from this belief? If you do not believe this moral or do not act from this belief, just reflect for a moment about why this might be and whether anything in your life, or your leadership style and activities, would be different if you did? Is there another moral that stands out to you in Andrew's story?

We have only identified nine areas from Andrew's narrative, although there are clearly many more. We have explored some of the other aspects of Andrew's narrative in the narratives of the other police officers in this book. Even then, there are aspects we do not touch on. What other elements of Andrew's narrative do you draw from and feel are of relevance in the development of greater resilience and to your development more generally? Why are these elements important, and how might you take these forward?

Case 4

8

Emotions on the Sidewalk
Ronald J. Walsh Jr

Introduction

I began my police career as a Special Agent with the US Department of Justice. The training here was exciting, the credentials impressive, and yet the job was at best lackluster, more paperwork and filing than police work; not for me. Inside I was seeking something that would help to "rush life to me," to create a feeling of being more "worldly" and experienced. Sitting behind a desk filing paperwork that effectuated arrests as opposed to finding the criminal and physically locking them up was simply not satisfying for me.

So after two years of being a Federal Agent, I quit and joined the New York Police Department (NYPD). I was originally assigned to walk a beat on the lower east side of Manhattan—a drug-infested area where nobody, at least no one who I ran across in my first twelve months on patrol, wanted to see a cop. Life for me then exposed me to hate, tragedy, pain, suffering, homelessness, drug addicts, drug dealers, murders, drunks, disease, despair, and the awful side of the human condition. I spent exactly three years with the NYPD—three years that helped me to know exactly how I did not want to work, live, or wind up. I used to say about my experience there that it was for the most part one where the people hated the cops, the cops hated the people, the police department hated the cops, and many of the cops hated each other. At the time I could see changes happening in me, changes I knew were not who I was; confusion and inner turmoil began to manifest. I was becoming bitter, bigoted, and filled with anger and mistrust. I knew that if I did not get out of there, and soon, I was going to become something that I just could not live with, something that my spirit did not have planned for me.

In 1992, nearly three years to the day from when I joined the NYPD, I joined the Nassau County Police Department. I graduated from the academy as class Valedictorian—the number one graduate. This was something I had also done at the NYPD, where out of the 1,300 recruit officers, I graduated as class Valedictorian and had the highest overall academic average as well. Not bad for a learning-disabled, stupid, hyperactive kid who would "never graduate from anything but a vocational training program," but that's another story for another day.

Nassau County was (and is) a much better environment for me. One of the reasons becoming Valedictorian became a goal for me was because the only person who was guaranteed to be assigned to their precinct of choice was the number one graduate, or someone who had a "hook" high enough to get them assigned to the precinct they wanted (a hook is a person who works in the police department who either is or has friends in high enough places that can "make a call" and have you assigned to any place you want). I did not have a hook, so Valedictorian was my only way. Being assigned to where I wanted was a big motivation, but to say it was my sole motivation would be overly simplifying. I was instilled with a belief from a very young age that I could do anything, and that if you told me I could not do, have, or be something, well that was all I needed to hear—step aside, because here comes the "bull in the china shop," I am going to get, do, or be exactly what I was told I could not get, do, or be.

The Parking Meter

I recall this incident vividly, and every time I think about it, I see it play out in my mind's eye. I was on patrol in a wealthy suburb of New York City (NYC). I was assigned to Post 401 (the patrol car number), which was a mixed residential and retail area, wealthy, and for the most part the residents were Jewish white-collar professionals. I was driving around my post when a call was transmitted over the radio. The call came over the airwaves something like the following: "401: respond to [location], in front of "The Gap," for a male and female black, attempting to break into parking meters. Be advised that the subjects are on the corner of [location]."

The day was hot and humid, it was late summer, I remember the air was heavy and dense; the kind of day where you wish you could stay in an air-conditioned room, or be lounging under a shady tree and not move. It was a Saturday, and the streets were very crowded with cars and angry traffic; people were walking, going from store to store shopping; lots of hustle and bustle. I was assigned. I responded back to headquarters (HQ), "401 responding; I'm only a couple of blocks from that location; check and advise." This meant that I would respond to the call, and my assisting car did not have to rush to the location since I was close, and I would "check and advise" if I needed them to respond.

It took less than a minute for me to drive to the location. There was lots of vehicle traffic, and the street was lined with retail stores on both sides. The stores were considered upscale, as was the neighborhood; both were considered "safe." As I was responding, HQ transmitted more complete details about the subjects:

> 401, be advised, the male black is approximately 6 feet 2 inches — 6 feet 4 inches, weighing approximately 250 pounds, wearing jeans, a brown shirt, a black "do-rag" covering his head, black mustache and beard, and has a hanger in his hand; the female is wearing a red shirt, blue pants, carrying white plastic bags; she has long, black, curly, braided hair, approximately 5 feet 7 inches, 150 pounds.

I was getting close to the corner.

As I made the left turn onto the street, I observed the two exactly where the radio said they would be, wearing exactly what I was told they would be wearing. The male was hunched over a little, and he was obviously struggling with something—pulling, lots of movement. All I could clearly see was his back, he was obviously working hard on something, and he was practically on top of the parking meter. I could see the end of a coat hanger wiggling around in the air, the other end obviously engaged in some sort of "business." It appeared to me that he was trying to get into the parking meter The female was standing with her back to his, looking around as if to see that nobody snuck up on them, I could see her eyes darting from side to side; she appeared concerned. I pulled down the block some distance, told HQ that I had arrived at the scene, and exited my police car. I could no longer see them from where I parked. I pulled far enough down the street as to be out of their view, tactically giving me the element of surprise. The two of them were about 20 feet west of the corner. I walked close to the building line, so they would not have the opportunity to see me and run; I would be upon them as soon as I reached the corner. As I rounded the turn, I called out to them, saying something to the effect, "Hey, can I help you with something?" Now, you have to imagine me at the time, 260 pounds of muscle (I was a competitive power lifter and was preparing for another competition), in full uniform, shaved head, calling to them in a powerful voice (my son says I have "the voice of Zeus, the God of Thunder"). While I was not quite yelling, I clearly was projecting my voice in a bounding way to emphasize control and authority.

The man spun his head around, the woman locked eyes on me, and both saw who I was. I read fear, surprise, shock, and they both knew immediately I was talking to them. The man appeared very agitated and angry, hyped up as if itching for a fight. He looked me square in the eyes as I quickly made my approach. The man immediately began a loud and very abusive verbal attack on me, yelling profanity that would have made a street walker blush, things to the effect of, "What, a f—ing black man can't be on the street in a f—ing white neighborhood? F—ing white cop come to chase the N—er away! What the f—k are you going to do?" Needless to say, I went right back at him, bellowing and becoming very hyped up: "Put your hands where I can see them, step away from the meter. Show me your hands. Keep your hands where I can see them, both of you." I kept telling him to keep his hands where I could see them. I told, basically ordered, the woman to take her bags, put them down, and to keep her hands where I could see them. My senses were heightened, pulse up, heartbeat pounding in my chest, readying for a fight. My mind was racing a little: why would he be so hostile toward me if he were doing nothing wrong? He is big! Careful, there are two of them. Position yourself so you can defend, don't get too close. Watch their hands, that is what can hurt you. I was getting pretty amped up. In police work, you come to recognize certain types of behavior, and over time and with experience you become very skeptical and always on high alert. Usually, if someone is this aggressive it is a distraction, something to get you to doubt what you are doing, something to get you to back off, to try and get you to make a mistake and to be afraid.

I moved the man from the parking meter, and got physical control of him … and then it happened. I could not believe it … the irate man who had been yelling and screaming at me from the second I got onto the scene was legitimate, he was doing nothing wrong! As the situation played out, I was able to ascertain during our verbal jousting that the couple had locked their keys in their car and he was just trying to unlock the car and get on his way. As it turned out, he was using the hangar to try and get into the car, not the meter. The situation, though, never calmed down, the man and woman both very angrily verbalized that they felt that the only reason I was talking to them was because they were black in a white neighborhood. In my anger, I told him where I thought he "should go," and further explained that it was not exactly the highlight of my day talking to them either, and that I had been called there by someone who thought they were "breaking into the God-dammed parking meter!" or something like that. I may have been more explicit. "What, you think I want to talk to you, like this is making my day?" I shouted as I turned, walked back to my police car and drove away. Only as I drove away it hit me. I did not get 10 feet from the curb when I found myself saying, "Well, that didn't go very well." Even through my anger I knew that things could not be left to stand as they were, I could not let that man and woman think that I am the way he now thinks I am, the way he assumed I was before I ever arrived. I was not going to let him go home and tell that story, that way, and perpetuate that paradigm. So I drove around the block, a very short distance that took only a few moments. I can only describe it as the way you feel just before the dentist begins drilling your teeth: anxiety, even though you know it is necessary. I pulled up to them again.

As I exited the car, I could see the defensive positioning and attitude, I could feel the anger and hatred, I could see the fury, and I could see his lungs beginning to fill with air so he could yell. It took everything I had to put myself in a place of forgiveness. I just raised my hands, both of them out in front of my body, in sort of a double "stop," I closed my eyes in a gesture of peace and surrender, and said in a soft and easy tone:

> *Just give me a moment here. I came back to say that what I did was wrong and I am sorry. I should not have lost my cool like that, and I just want you to know that if you need a tow truck or a locksmith, I will call one for you.*

On this hot, humid day, on the busy suburban street, with all the people and cars and trucks and noise and everything else that goes along with a major retail shopping area on a blistering summer Saturday, you could have heard a pin drop. Everything fell away in that moment. All the hate, the prejudice, the anger; it all just simply melted away for all of us. Time stood still for a moment on that avenue, and there was peace and understanding between the three of us—a peace that represented something that I never thought could happen so fast, a spiritual intercession that spoke to me like never before. I learned in that moment that peace is possible, that love, forgiveness, and understanding will triumph, that God, or spirit or the connective force that I always knew existed in the universe was in us all. We shook hands, his door opened, we both went on into the world to tell our stories. We both knew. Funny, though, it took me years to tell anyone this story. Maybe I was just not ready.

Every day as police officers we come to work to protect and serve a public that many times not only does not appreciate us, but also accuses us of being cruel and unjust in the way we carry out our assigned duties. The unexplainable feelings of dismay and betrayal that accompany the accusations thrust upon you when you were doing your best to help only serve to weaken the already fragile balance within us as beings. The denunciations that you never expected to have to deal with at the time, somewhere down the road become, well, expected, which is sad if you take the time to think about it.

As a profession, we are under constant scrutiny and held to a higher standard, and we should be. We know better than the general public what is right and wrong, at least as far as the law goes, and we are sworn to protect and serve, to uphold the constitution (in the US) and the laws of our respective states. If you ever take the time to truly observe, you will soon realize that many of us feel so isolated and alienated from normal society that we can only relate to other officers, clearly showing that we feel as if nobody else is capable of understanding us. Often times we do not trust our departments, feeling that they are out to get us, to make examples of us for doing our jobs the best and only way we knew how to at the time. As a group, we feel that "our families just would not understand how we feel," and that we cannot turn to them because "they just don't get it." The us versus them syndrome leads to feelings of resentment, apathy, mistrust, cynicism, hopelessness, and desperation.

It is important to realize that everything that we as people do, no matter how small, no matter how insignificant we believe it may be, changes the world in some small way. Edward Lorenz, a US mathematician and meteorologist, is well known for the notion of the "Butterfly Effect," the idea that a small disturbance, like the flapping of a butterfly's wings, can induce enormous consequences. Lorenz's theory cannot be proved yet, since we do not have the technological ability (yet) to gather the quantity of information it would take to know everything in the universe that could possibly affect the atmosphere at any given moment in time. However, if you accept Lorenz's theory, then everything we do as individuals could somehow change the world in some small (or large) way. Take, for instance, my example in this narrative on the way I handled the encounter with the man and woman who had locked their keys in their car by accident. Had I decided to leave that scene and not return, leaving behind all the ill will and anger, then perhaps the following might have been the continuation of that story:

The man and woman manage to get into their car and go about their day. Clearly affected by what happened, they finally get home, where they find that their children are acting up, being loud, playful, like all children, only today mom and dad had a bad day. They take out their anger on the kids, yelling at them, punishing them, and overreacting to their otherwise harmless play. Later, some friends and family come over for dinner. The story is told of the bigoted white cop who abused them because they were black and on the street in the lily-white neighborhood. The anger and resentment builds, the hatred locks in, and over time, the children learn. Time passes, years go by, and in some small part that encounter plays a role in forming a hatred for the police in the children, only to be reinforced by the experiences told by their friends, and their neighbors and family.

One day, the children are grown adults out in the world. One of them finds himself out one night, driving in not such a great neighborhood. A cop pulls him over, it's dark, raining a little, isolated feel to the road. Unknown to the young man, his left brake light is out and the officer is thinking about writing a summons, but as he has been taught, he is ever vigilant and realizes that traffic stops are some of the most dangerous duties an officer carries out. The officer knows why he is pulling the man over, but the officer does not know if he has stopped a man who has just robbed a bank, beaten his wife, or lost his father to cancer. The police officer may be running into just about anything, and he needs to be ready for anything to take place. The officer walks up to the car, the young black man refuses to open his window. The officer's antenna wiggles, he feels something strange, the energy here, there is something just not right. This certainly is not the first time he has pulled someone over who refused to roll down their window; there is just something different this time, but what?

The young man in the car is seething, his hatred for the oppression is boiling over, in his mind all he was doing was driving down the street, trying to get to a friend's party, he was in a great mood; now, though, he is full of hate, full of fear that he may become the victim just like his family and friends warned him, just like his parents had been years before. Finally, he rolls down the window, the hatred flows from within, he yells at the officer, the officer instinctively goes into defense mode, the officer thinks, "Protect yourself, watch his hands, hands, blade your stance, make yourself a smaller target, be ready." The man is more than rude, he is abusive.

All of a sudden, the man in the car in a fit of anger reaches under the front seat; the officer yells, "SHOW ME YOUR HANDS!" The man, furious, sees this as the officer now trying to control his movements, take his freedom, his rights and he knows he has done nothing wrong. The officer backs up two feet, screaming, "SHOW ME YOUR HANDS! DON'T MOVE! SHOW ME YOUR HANDS!"

The young man comes up with something in his hands, something bulky, a glint of steel reflects off the slight illumination provided by the street light; the officer cannot believe he may be killed, he thinks "Gun, gun, he has a gun." Quickly, without thinking, he ducks to the side out of the way ever so slightly; perceiving what he knows to be a gun, he draws, fires one shot at the vehicle, the bullet crushes into the temple of the young black man in the front seat of his car; the young man, his last thought as his mind goes blank, "I knew this would happen some day!"

The officer calls for backup, shots fired, shots fired, frenzy. As his backup shows up at the scene, the officers begin to approach the subject's vehicle, caution rules the day, shouts of "SHOW ME YOUR HANDS! PUT YOUR HANDS OUT THE WINDOW! SHOW ME YOUR HANDS," yelled over and over and over. As the officers finally reach the vehicle, it becomes obvious that the man in the car will never show his hands again. His lifeless body is slumped over the center console. The officers check for a pulse; they request an ambulance. The search for the weapon begins; all that is found, clutched in his hands, is a bulky, black wallet with a shiny chrome zipper. He was unarmed, he was angry and yelling, and the fear was so thick you could actually smell it, feel it, taste it; but no gun. The officer, in shock, cannot believe what just happened. The investigation begins. The world, the universe has changed. The Butterfly Effect—the smallest actions of a single person can change the world, only you may never know what you avoided, in all probability you will never be able to parse out the difference your actions may have made in the world. All you can do is the best you can. And sometimes that means driving around a short block, which is the longest trip you have ever taken, to change what may never be known.

The Fishing Trip

In another powerful experience I recall as if it were yesterday, I was in an unmarked police car and doing traffic enforcement for the day with my partner. We were standing on the double yellow lines that separated traffic, enforcing inspection, registration, and seatbelt violations. As the morning went on, I remember seeing a real "jalopy" car driving toward me. It was an early 1970s Ford stationwagon with the simulated wood panels on the side. Rusty, and all beat up. I could see that there were at least two people in the car. As the vehicle came closer, I could see that both the inspection and registration had expired and neither of the front passengers were wearing their seatbelts. I put my hand out as an authoritative STOP signal. The car stopped, and I told the driver to pull into an adjacent parking lot. I was thinking that my enforcement worries were solved. This car was going to end the need for me to have to stand out in traffic that day because I would be able to get at least five or six summonses on this one stop.

As I approached the driver's side door and began speaking with the man, I quickly realized that this traffic stop was not going to be routine, not at all. The driver of the car was an elderly African American, in his seventies, weathered skin, bent fingers, dry, ashy, calloused hands, plain white T-shirt, a little dirty, wisdom emanating from within; his friend sitting next to him was of the same vintage. The interior of the car was all beat up, the seat's upholstery was worn and tattered, the glove box held closed with duct tape, the rear of the car filled with assorted garbage, buckets, fishing poles, blankets, old newspapers, all sorts of stuff from years of collection. Out of sheer rote I asked him for his license, registration, and insurance card. The man greeted me with a kind, nervous voice.

As he was searching for his paperwork, I asked the man where he was heading. He replied, "Goin' fishin' down by the bridge to catch some dinner." The man spoke with a southern inflection in his voice. He handed me his paperwork, all of which was expired, I will never forget the feeling that I got when my eyes met his for an ever so brief moment. I immediately realized that this man had been subjected to the worst that mankind could dish out. I could see the nervous anxiety in his heart, and I could feel the trepidation that was in his every reply and mannerism.

I could hear and feel, by the way he was answering me, that he had learned his lessons in the past, and that he was not going to look at me too long in the eyes, nor answer me in any way that I could interpret as challenging or disrespectful. I knew instinctively that these two men were going to do exactly what they said they were going to do: they were going to go down to the bridge and catch some dinner. Maybe some of the reason was for entertainment, friendship, but there certainly was the necessity to eat, and I am positive that sustenance was the greater role and motivation for their fishing expedition. I told the man to wait in his car.

I turned and yelled to my partner to come over, and we both went and sat down in our unmarked patrol car. I sat in the car and told my partner what I had, and that we were going to have to pack up for now. He asked me why.

I explained to him that there was no way that I could issue this man a ticket. I explained that there are some times when the greater good is served by exercising discretion, and that this was one of them. We both realized that issuing the summonses that could have been issued that day would have been legitimate and legal, that is certain, but being legal does not always mean correct, nor does it have to be hurtful. I figured that we could accomplish the same results by handling the situation in a more compassionate and spiritual way. I went back to the car and handed the man his paperwork.

I explained to him that while I could not allow him to drive away, I had to leave at that moment. I explained that I was fairly new to the area and that I had at least twenty more years before I retired, and that I patrolled the area every day, and that next time the situation would have to be handled in a different way. I explained much more without words that day than I ever could have with them, because when I handed that man his paperwork, I immediately felt a sense of astonishment and disbelief coupled with an overriding sense of kindness and forgiveness; the man was shocked, to say the least. I never saw that man or his friend again, but I know in my heart that the events of that day not only affected me, but also clearly affected the driver and passenger in the most positive and spiritual ways. I can only imagine the stories that were told at his kitchen table that night. Somehow I feel as if I was able to restore just a little faith in mankind that day, and for me it was one of the high points of my career. Funny, though, no award, no accolade—just me knowing that on that day I served God, and helped make the world a better place. Perhaps I simply chose to perceive the situation in the way I am reflecting it here today. Perhaps. But as a result, I know I grew, I felt it happen; I felt the spirit of the world rising inside me, screaming to me that this is why you are here, right now. Watch the butterflies soar.

Individuals can change the world. The realization that no matter how good or not so good you are (or think you are), you, we can all change and become better. Manage your life and intentions to reflect and achieve excellence in life's big challenges by developing the habit of excellence in all small things. Excellence in your life should not be the exception, it should become your destiny. I evolve, every moment, shifting, transforming into who I see myself becoming. It is not projection toward the sky, but more like a winding mountain road, slow and gradual. There is no end, no final destination, there just is, and that becomes the art of being.

Leader Reflection

- What stands out for you in this narrative regarding resilience?
- What elements of this narrative link to the aspects of resilience you are working with?
- What other elements of the narrative are important to you, and why?

9

Emotions on the Sidewalk: Analysis

There are some powerful messages in Ron's narrative that speak for themselves. There are also a number of elements we have discussed in previous chapters, particularly Chapters 1 and 3: the spiritual aspects to the experience, reflections, emotions, connections, time slowing down or standing still, and extraordinary experiences are some of these.

In this analysis, we would like to focus on another seven aspects which we feel are significant in the development of resilience.

Influence of Experience

We see several examples in Ron's narrative of a cycle of emotions taking place, as we depict in Figure 9.1.

In both of Ron's interactions described in his narrative – at the parking meter and the fishing trip – we see the cycle in Figure 9.1 played out. The experience we are having impacts directly on our emotions, which influences our attitude, which guides our behaviour, which impacts on the experience we are having, and so the cycle continues. Can you identify this cycle in Ron's narrative? Can you think of situations when you have experienced this cycle taking place? What was the outcome of this, and what impact did the cycle have?

This is not the full story, however, and as is clearly shown in Ron's narrative, we almost always have at least one other person involved in the process. This results in another cycle starting, as depicted in Figure 9.2.

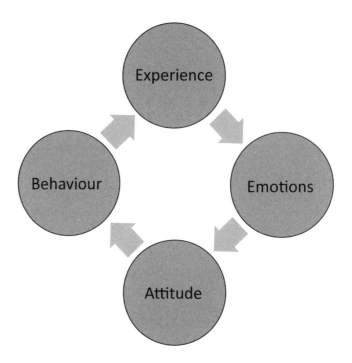

Figure 9.1   The Cycle of Emotions

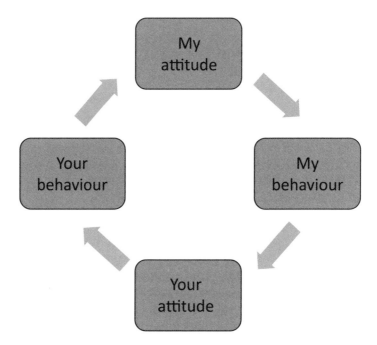

Figure 9.2   Cycle impacting on another

Whilst models are always simplifications of reality – they have to be, otherwise they would be so complicated we could never understand them – we hope Figures 9.1 and 9.2 shed some light on the interactions we can all have. These cycles in Figures 9.1 and 9.2 are perhaps more accurately represented as spirals rather than cycles. In the parking meter experience in Ron's narrative, Ron shows that these spirals can either be negative spirals downwards, with the situation getting worse and worse, or we can have positive spirals upwards, where things are gradually improving.

Are you in one of these spirals? If so, which way is it going, and what impact is it having? Why?

It would seem logical that we are likely to be more resilient if these spirals in our lives are positive upward spirals. But is it really possible to change the direction of the spiral from downwards negative to upwards positive? Ron's narrative would strongly suggest it is. The research on Emotional Intelligence would also indicate it is possible to change the direction of the spirals. What do you think? Is it possible for you to change any of the negative spirals you are experiencing? If it is, at which stage in Figures 9.1 and 9.2 do you feel it is best to do this?

Influence of Policing

In this narrative, Ron talks about the impact policing in Manhattan was having on him, where the "people hated the cops, the cops hated the people, the police department hated the cops, and many of the cops hated each other". He said he could see he was becoming "bitter, bigoted, and filled with anger and mistrust". It is very clear that this type of organizational environment was wearing away Ron's resilience.

Why might it get to this position within the police? It is clearly a complex situation, but Ron's narrative may give us some insights to assist our appreciation of some of the dynamics that may be at play here, which can increase our understanding of factors in the workplace which can impact on our resilience.

Firstly, as Ron indicates, much of police work is dangerous and uncertain, and how an officer copes with this almost continuous threat is significant. There are a huge variety of different types of duties seen in operational police work, and some of these, as we see in Andrew's narrative in Chapter 6, come under the category of exercising control over the perpetrators of criminal activity, including dealing with violent criminals and public order situations. Other duties, as we see in Ron's narrative, come under the category of care, including dealing with victims of crime and vulnerable witnesses. These are very different roles, yet the same police officer may be required to perform these different duties many times in the same shift. The different roles raise questions about the role of the police in society: should they be agents of social control – a police force – or a police service? Whilst Fielding and Conroy (1994: 193) identify with both roles, they feel that the overwhelming ethos of the police is as a force. This seems hardly surprising when so much of a police officer's contact with the public, as we see in both Ron's narrative and Andrew's in Chapter 6, can be tainted by, or threatens to escalate towards, aggressive or violent behaviour. In such circumstances, officers want, and are trained, to always try to be in control and to always have the advantage over the aggressor, since a failure to do so may lead to attacks on either the officers involved or on others. However, Perez and Shtull argue that often this is taken too far, and the police are: "fixated with situation control as a critical sub-cultural norm, and cling to the idea of 'staying invincible' and avoiding closeness to people and their problems" (Perez and Shtull 2002: 174).

Stephens and Becker argue also that the police are really a quasi-military organization, indicated by the strong hierarchical command structure that is in place, premised: "not just on the basis of controlling disorder and crime among the public but also on controlling its own officers" (Stephens and Becker 1994: 221).

With threat and danger ever present, it is easy to understand why police officers want to be in control. However, this effort to be in control all the time can be extremely draining, and as Green and Humphrey (2012: 66) highlight, is one of the major underlying causes of stress. The observation by Perez and Shtull (2002: 174) also raises the question as to whether the continual effort for control is necessary within the police environment, or whether it goes too far much of the time.

People desire such control in their lives so that they know what is happening and what they are doing. Feeling out of control can be very stressful, and can mean you can be just knocked from one crisis to the next and feel you never achieve what you want to. In the work environment, people can feel a lack of control from such things as high workloads and major change programmes, and these can be major sources of stress, according to Green and Humphrey (2012: 66).

With the continual change and uncertainty, as well as the complexity of the global environment today, it is simply impossible to be in control of everything. Also, it may be that the fear of feeling completely out of control means we overreact and try and control things too tightly to guard against this. However, employees may expect leaders to be in control and know everything, and may see them as weak if they do not appear to be. This raises a number of questions for you:

- Do you try to keep control?

- Do you try to convey the impression to employees that you are in control?

- Are you honest with them about the things you are in control of, and the things you are not? If not, why is this, and what are the implications?

Focusing now on the issue of control for you personally, how do you feel about the need to be in control? What things do you feel the need to be in control of? Is this necessary? What are the implications of this for you? What other aspects of control can you identify? Do you feel you achieve an appropriate and manageable balance between control and empowering your employees, between your controlling things and your allowing them to take the control and move things in the direction they feel is appropriate? What might be the impact on you and your employees' resilience if you did delegate this control and empower them more?

A lot of the police research emphasizes this issue of desire for control, but in Ron's narrative we see a very different picture of policing. Why is this? Is Ron, or the area, department, or country where he works, very different to the norm? Or is it that these stories shared by Ron are actually very different from the norm experienced by Ron, and stand out and are recounted because of this? Are these stories really more examples of how Ron would like policing to be as the norm or thinks it perhaps could be?

If it were the case that the stories shared with us by Ron were very different from the norm and were more examples of how Ron thinks more of policing could or should be, then what might the effect of this difference be on police officers? We saw in Smith and Charles (2010) that police officers typically enter the police profession with a desire to do something meaningful, to help others, to make a positive contribution to their community and wider society, as Ron demonstrates in his narrative. However, both Charles (2005) and Smith (2005) found that when working on the streets as an operational officer, some participants in their research said they experienced a sharp contrast between this desire and the realities of operational policing. Within weeks of joining, new recruits realize that the job is more about confrontation and crisis than anything else, as Ron talks about in Manhattan – dealing with people who hate you for no specific reason, feeling unappreciated, and where you are often ostracized, and mentally or physically abused. In such situations, there can be a role conflict for police officers between their desire to make a difference, to help others and make a positive contribution, and the realities described above. We argue that this role conflict may be one of the reasons why the resilience of police officers can be eroded. Faced with this conflict, some police officers can lose themselves in anger, succumb to the pressures on the street, or become bitter or cynical, as Ron identifies in the narrative, and as also do Carlier (1999), Figley (1999), and Violanti and Paton (1999).

We argue that a similar situation can be experienced in leadership positions more generally, but this is even less recognized, researched, or discussed. Often, leaders take on roles believing that they can make a difference, can make a positive contribution to society, and can help people, only to find that they are dragged down by bureaucracy, paperwork, workload, or a negative organizational culture. What affect does this have on leaders and their resilience, and how do they cope with this? Do you experience this at all? If so, what affect does it have on you, and how do you cope with this?

So often when you are caught up in this type of situation and the downward negative spiral that results (Figures 9.1 and 9.2), it is not easy to see that you are changing, and you become more and more bitter and angry. Even when friends and family tell you this, you do not see it, you blame them, and you think it is they who have changed, not you. The downward negative spiral continues until it is too late: "Every day in America one police officer reaches the point where he [sic] feels his life no longer has meaning, and he tragically kills himself" (Smith and Charles 2010: 321).

So how do you spot and stop this negative downward spiral early, and then reverse it into a positive upward spiral? How does Ron do this? It may be, as in Ron's case, that there is no option but to leave the organization. Some people may not have this option, however, and this can also be a huge loss for the organization. Leaders have a responsibility to examine and change a negative organizational culture, and if they do this, it can be of huge benefit to themselves, their employees, and the organization as a whole, and can have positive knock-on effects in the wider community. Training is an important element within this change process. In the policing context, we argue that for this training to be effective, however, it has to be undertaken before officers get drawn into that downward negative spiral that can make them bitter, bigoted, and filled with anger and mistrust. That means when officers first join the service. Smith and Charles (2010) make a number of proposals for the range of training that is required to address these areas, and emphasize the importance of adopting a holistic approach and including training for family, police supervisors, and managers.

What about leaders more generally, where in our experience these negative impacts and cultural issues are often not recognized and training is rarely provided on these areas to support and guide? If training is not available, having an awareness of the issue is certainly one of the first major steps in assisting leaders, and we hope this book will help you with this. Another useful technique is to utilize reflective practice, as we saw in Wendy's narrative in Chapter 4 and discussed in Chapters 5 and 7. This embedding of a reflective practice approach is a relatively easy and cheap strategy that can assist in building resilience, and it is something that people can do for themselves. It is a strategy embedded in many organizations, including the professional body for the Human Resource profession, the Chartered Institute for Personnel and Development (CIPD),[1] and the National Health Service (NHS).[2]

In the narrative, we see Ron reflecting on the situation almost as soon as he walks away from the people he encountered at the parking meter. He recalls thinking, "Well that didn't go very well." He obviously goes further than just thinking that, however, and completes the Experiential Learning Cycle we discussed in Chapter 5. It is clear that he reflects quickly on the consequences of the interaction and the implications if he leaves the encounter as it is. He addresses the "Now What?" element, and decides to return to the scene and apologies. This had tremendous positive outcomes, according to Ron, and we can only speculate on all the long-term positive repercussions of his actions on that hot and humid summer day by that parking meter in New York City.

---

1   See http://www.cipd.co.uk/cpd.
2   See http://www.flyingstart.scot.nhs.uk/learning-programmes/reflective-practice.aspx.

Decision-making

Another important aspect in Ron's narrative is connected to decision-making. We will focus here on the fishing trip element of the narrative. Ron clearly had to make a decision about what to do when the car stopped and he saw the men in the car. As is typical in policing, he also had to make this decision quickly. Although this is not a text on decision-making, making decisions can sometimes be a difficult and stressful experience, and in seeking to assist leaders develop their resilience, it may be worth taking a few moments to explore some of the issues and processes involved in doing this. It will also be worth examining the things leaders and organizations may be able to do to ease the burden of decision-making on people in the organization. Organizations have a responsibility to ease this decision-making burden as much as possible to protect their employees from undue stress, while still allowing their employees the freedom and autonomy to make the right decisions. If they can achieve an appropriate balance here, then they will be building a system which is inherently more resilient.

This raises a very interesting side question which we will just identify here, but you may wish to reflect on further: What systems and processes could you develop further in your organization that would build an organization that is inherently more resilient?

In police and leadership decision-making more generally, what seems key in terms of our focus on developing leadership resilience is that people feel happy and at ease with the decisions they have made, and can sleep easily in their beds at night after having made a decision. This is clearly the case for Ron. We would argue that if leaders make decisions and then are constantly worrying whether they were the right ones, or are having to spend a considerable amount of time justifying their decisions to themselves, colleagues, the organization, other employees, and the public, it is likely to have a considerably detrimental effect on leaders' long-term well being, energy, and resilience.

Let's examine for a moment the decisions Ron is making in the fishing trip element of his narrative. In this situation, if he was rigidly sticking to a set procedure then it would be very easy, as there is then only a straightforward decision to be made – are the driver's documents valid and up to date, or not? If they are not, then the procedure tells him clearly what he would do next. This is a simple binary logic – valid or not, right or wrong. Of course, in policing and in the majority of leadership activities, the situation is never that easy, and not all the factors impacting on the decision are the same each time. To deal with the complexities Ron finds himself dealing with, it is important, as Ron does, to draw on the aspect of police officer discretion. As soon as you introduce this discretion, however, the decision-making process and policies are much more complicated for the officer concerned, and also for the police service in terms of initial training and in ensuring some form of consistency and checks on the decisions police officers are making. We can clearly see Ron using his discretionary powers to good effect in the fishing trip story, and this led to a very positive and long-lasting impact for Ron, and most likely for the two men in the car as well as their friends, family, and community.

But let us probe the process involved in Ron's decisions a little further. In the narrative, it seems clear that for the people in the car going on that fishing trip, Ron's decision that day was a good one and would help to build their trust and confidence in the police. It was also likely to do the same for the friends, family, and communities connected to the two men in the car. However, could there be other groups where trust and confidence might be reduced as a result of Ron's decisions? What about people who struggle to find money to pay for the relevant documents for their car but nevertheless pay these bills regularly? Whilst Ron's decisions are spirit-warming and sound nice, would they stand up to public scrutiny? Of course, we have the luxury here of hindsight and time to reflect on the issues and look at all possible options. Ron only had a few minutes to talk with the car's occupants and to have a brief discussion with his colleague.

When Ron made the decisions described in the narrative, what was he basing these decisions on? – no doubt, procedure and the law, previous decisions he and his colleague had made as well as the outcomes of these. However, was there something more, deeper in Ron's psyche, that would also influence the decisions he made that day? Did his upbringing, his history, his schooling and culture come into play? Did his values and beliefs influence things on that morning as he stood on those double white lines in front of that rusty and beat-up old Ford stationwagon? If these later aspects do influence our decision-making, then these seem important aspects for leaders and organizations to consider in terms of ensuring consistency and fairness, and in providing the appropriate training on effective decision-making.

Lee (as discussed in Howard and Smith 2011) is instrumental within the UK police service in trying to develop a framework for decision-making to try to assist officers with this complex and difficult task. He focuses on a values-based approach to decision-making (VBDM). One of his VBDM models that is discussed in Howard and Smith (2011) is shown in Figure 9.3.

Step 7: Monitor and review – be prepared to
be flexible.
Step 6: Decide, act and record.
Step 5: If in doubt – consult.
Step 4: Check your decision would stand public scrutiny.
Step 3: Choose the best option to build trust and confidence.
Step 2: Consider options based on force values.
Step 1: Know the law or regulations.

Figure 9.3   Value-Based Decision Making Model (VBDM)

Source: Lee in Howard and Smith (2011).

This model is an attempt to provide police officers with a framework for making decisions which aims to ease their burden, and is an example of an organization trying to embed a system of decision-making into its policies and procedures so that the organization is inherently more resilient. Lee (in Howard and Smith 2011) claims that the values-based model is helpful: for officers, in that it supports the development of professional judgement and encourages discretionary leadership, and for the organization, in that it helps the police to drive the day-to-day business of policing from a strong values base.

In the UK police, this VBDM model has been developed into the National Decision Model (NDM), which can be seen in Figure 9.4.

The VBDM model in Figure 9.3 requires forces to have a clear set of values that officers can base their decisions on (Step 2 in Figure 9.3). In the NDM shown in Figure 9.4, values are at the centre of the model and are covered by the *Statement of Mission and Values for the Police Service* (ACPO 2011). This statement includes:

- Make communities safer by upholding the law fairly and firmly.

- Act with integrity, compassion, courtesy, and patience.

- Show neither fear nor favour in what you do.

- Be sensitive to the needs and dignity of victims.

- Demonstrate respect for the human rights of all.

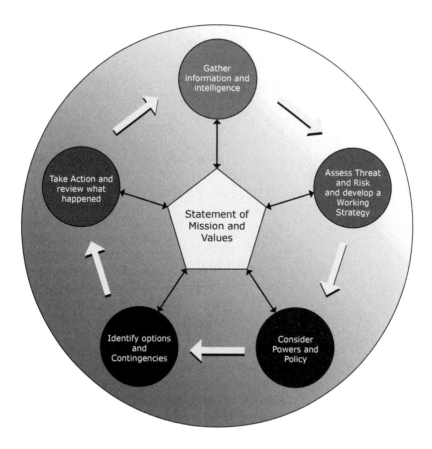

Figure 9.4   The UK police's National Decision Model (NDM)
Source: Adapted from ACPO (2012).

- Use discretion, professional judgement, and common sense to guide you.

- Be accountable for decisions and actions.

Hufton (2013) is currently exploring the area of police decision-making in his research. His thesis proposes that routine police decision-making is perilously difficult when considered in depth, and is more complex that the above models suggest. The multiple paradoxes and contradictions of the operating environment of policing provide a level of complexity that defies "rationality". The difficulty here, though, is that the judicial operating environment as well as the police processes and procedures require decisions to be justified using only logic that would pass the test of "a reasonable person". As we have said above, and seen in

Ron's narrative, the main principle of police decision-making is that it frequently involves making judgements that are based on discretion. Hufton argues, as we have seen in Ron's decisions, that this discretion is actually formed of a unique mix of pre-conscious thought with an amalgam of circumstance, law, policy, practice, and procedure, all of which are tainted with personal values, cultural norms, and peer pressures. This all means, Hufton argues, that the required test by the reviewing "reasonable person" would never be able to replicate the circumstances of the decision, so all policing decisions are, by definition, unique and non-replicable. The complication with all this is that it actually puts the police officer in a difficult, challenging, and vulnerable position: it makes the officer subject to scrutiny, because he or she can never be "right", as the actual situations are not matters of right and wrong, but balances of judgement and perspective. Hufton points out that despite this reality, officers are often required to defend their decisions as if they were "absolutely" right, leading to defensive reductionism and a tendency to over-state opinion and judgement as "fact". Hufton rightly points out that this is inherently stressful. Hufton (2013) is also exploring how officers cope with this regular sequence of stressful decision-making and justification events. He suggests that coping strategies based upon spirituality may be helpful to officers in these situations. He argues that officers may have greater resilience to cope where they seek to construe their work in terms of meaningful activity that contributes to positive societal outcomes – in essence, the larger purpose we discussed in Chapter 1 and will explore further in Chapters 13 and 15. This mechanism may be helpful, Hufton suggests, as it does not rely or dwell upon a micro-analysis of the situation, but allows officers to frame their work in terms of the larger goal of helping others. In short, Hufton is tentatively proposing that spirituality related to meaning-making may help strengthen a police officer's resolve and offer reassurance, potentially lowering stress factors and reinforcing coping strategies.

We would argue that leaders are frequently in situations where they too are required to make decisions based on their discretion, making their decisions much more difficult and more open to scrutiny. Often, however, this is not recognized, and leaders can be unaware of this whole decision-making process, and the influences that are impacting on it, because leaders are operating at the unconscious level with respect to decision-making.

Leaders develop their decision-making capabilities in the organizational context in which they operate over many years. They have probably progressed through the steps we identify in the Conscious Competence Ladder shown in Figure 9.5, which is a popular and intuitive explanation of how skills are developed which has been attributed to many different possible originators:

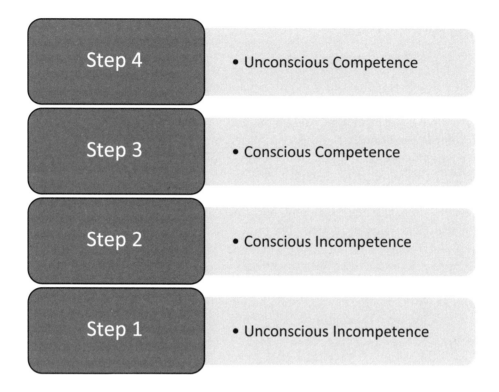

Figure 9.5   The Conscious Competence Ladder

You are probably making the vast majority of your decisions at the fourth level in Figure 9.5 – "Unconscious Competence". However, Mauboussin (2012: 49) argues that people's deep confidence in their judgements and abilities is often at odds with the reality. The processes you use to make decisions may actually be resulting in decisions that are creating difficulties for you, or you may unconsciously be following a process or procedure that cannot actually work effectively in practice. This could all be causing you or your employees stress and eroding your resilience.

What we invite you to do is to take a step back for a few moments, try to bring the decision-making processes you are following back to Step 3 in Figure 9.5 – "Conscious Competence" – and reflect on the appropriateness of these in your current situation. What influences your decision-making? What training have you had to enable you to make the best decisions? What does your organization do to guide and protect you as much as they are able in this area? Could the decision-making processes you follow be improved in any way? How do you know?

The Butterfly Effect

Ron talks of Edward Lorenz in his narrative. According to Chang (2008), Lorenz was partially responsible for popularizing the idea that a butterfly flapping its wings in Africa today may very well be the variable that causes a hurricane in Texas two years from now. Known more technically as "sensitive dependence on initial conditions", the theory is based on a mathematical model of the way air moves around in the atmosphere. Lorenz (cited in Chang 2008), while studying weather patterns, clearly realized that the weather and atmosphere did not always change as predicted. Minute variations in the initial conditions resulted in completely different outcomes in weather patterns, as shown through his computer models. The huge differences in weather patterns that resulted from very minute changes in the starting point of the computer model came to be known as the "Butterfly Effect". Lorenz showed that minute changes altered weather patterns, and he therefore concluded that in order to accurately predict weather patterns, one would have to know the precise reading of every possible atmospheric condition (everything that could possibly move or effect the air), and every possible thing that could cause a change in them throughout the world at a given moment would have to be known in order to accurately predict what the weather would be. Think how enormous a task it would be to know everything that could possibly move the air in the entire world.

The Butterfly Effect links to the systems thinking and holistic approaches we discussed in Chapter 1. It highlights the fact that all things are connected, and the possibility that our small actions today can have a massive effect some time in the future, even though we may not be able to predict what these are.

Childhood

Ron's narrative draws our attention to his childhood and the things that he was told and observed during that time. We suggest that a great many of the things we think and believe, and many of the ways in which we act as adults, come from our childhood. If this is the case, it may be extremely beneficial for us to reflect and question as we grow older how we were educated, socialized, and brought up when we were children, and whether our attitudes, beliefs, and behaviours that have come from our childhood are still appropriate for the time, situation, and culture we are now in. The influences from our childhood are summarized in the Embedded Values Cycle we discussed in Chapter 7. This cycle also identifies the tremendous influence we can have on the thoughts and views of the children we interact with and have in our care.

What is the message about leadership and resilience that you are giving through your actions and words to your children, or the children you interact with? Is this the message about life, leadership, and resilience that you want them to take forward with them?

Hypervigilance

In the potential follow-on scenario to the parking meter encounter in Ron's narrative, we see indications of what Gilmartin (2002: 33) identifies as "hypervigilance". Hypervigilance, according to Gilmartin, is the perceptual set of elevated alertness of the surroundings which is required of police officers for maximum officer safety. As we see in Ron's narrative, the necessity to be continually asking questions like "Is that person reaching for his wallet, or a gun?" is paramount if officers are to survive. According to Gilmartin (2002: 35), hypervigilance is the viewing of the world from a threat-based perspective, and having the mindset to see the events unfolding as potentially hazardous, which is necessary for police officers. Gilmartin (2002: 38) suggests that hypervigilance is a biological state with its foundation in the neurological functioning of the brain. The brain has a set of structures known as the reticular activating system (RAS) that determines the level of alertness that is necessary at any given time. Whenever the brain interprets the existence of a potential for threat or risk, the RAS engages the higher-functioning levels of the brain into a higher level of awareness and perceptiveness of the environment.

So when police officers are on duty, they operate above the normal range of alertness and awareness, as shown in Figure 9.6.

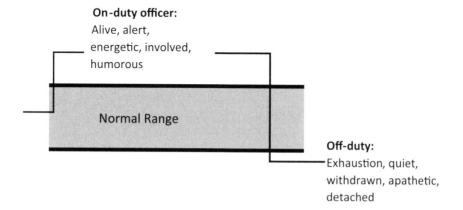

Figure 9.6   Levels of alertness for police officers

However, the body cannot cope with this heightened sense of awareness continually, and as Gilmartin (2002) discusses in detail, the result is that when police officers are off duty, their RAS swings to below the normal range of alertness in order to cope. This can have major implications for officers' relationships with their partners, family, and friends, as the officers communicate and socialize less and less and associate with the job more and more in order to experience all the positive emotions and alertness.

Gilmartin explores this for police officers, but we argue that leaders more generally can have very similar experiences. Although we would not term this "hypervigilance", but perhaps "hyperalertness", the feelings of being alive, alert, energetic, and involved when at work, the swing to below-average alertness when not working, and the negative impacts on family and friends can be very similar.

Impressions

Ron's narrative clearly highlights how easy it can be to form the wrong impression. People often make very quick judgements based on few or no facts, and only on the first impressions they form of individuals. Sometimes these first impressions are right, but often they can be found to be incomplete or wrong once more information has been collected, or when you get to know the individual better. For police officers, this can be particularly difficult because often they may not have time to gather more information or get to know the individual better, and have to make a quick decision or judgement, which can be in life or death situations, and which rely on these first impressions. Leaders can also form views of people from their first impressions. These may not involve the need to make such quick decisions, but leaders can make major decisions based on these first impressions just the same. Are the views you have of people overly based on the first impression you had of them? If so, why is this? What are the dangers of these first impressions, and what might you do to guard against letting these first impressions influence your actions inappropriately?

Isolation for Police Officers

Ron's narrative highlights the issue of isolation and the danger that police officers can become increasingly isolated by the roles they perform. Rees and Smith (2008: 1) argue that the work some police officers do, and the way in which they learn to live with this and the violent situations in which they frequently have to engage, can keep them in a constant state of alienation from the rest of society – in its shadow. The feeling of always being on duty was reported by many officers in Smith's research, and as the quotation below illustrates, the difficulties that can be experienced when off duty mean that many police officers tend to socialize with other officers:

> it is very much a closed community within the police service. People are always beating you up for this, that and the other, even when you're off duty, they know what you do for a living and it's difficult to perhaps break away from that ....

> (Smith 2005: 256)

This gravitating to other officers is understandable, as this is where you feel safe and feel you can perhaps relax for a moment.

Rees and Smith (2008) identify that as well as an individual response to danger, there is also a social response. When danger is signalled, people who are attached to each other feel compelled to draw together. This increased attachment behaviour in the face of danger or threat has been noted with all social species. As children, our only safety is to be found in the protection of others, and when fear is aroused, we seek protection from others, even when we are adults. In such conditions, Rees and Smith (2008) argue, we are also more obedient and open to suggestion. It also helps us to modulate each others' emotional responses and see the situation more clearly. Walker (1994) highlights that the nature of operational police work, with its danger and uncertainty, tends to bind officers to their immediate work group. However, Walker also points out the negative aspects of this group cohesiveness, which can result in insularity and defensive solidarity.

Smith and Charles (2010: 328) suggest that the situations police officers regularly experience can lead to feelings of isolation, and as a result officers can be suspicious of others and often find it difficult to disclose their feelings (a view supported by Kirschman 2006: 28). The police are sworn to protect the citizens of the community, yet those same citizens may also be the enemy (supported by Burbeck and Furnham 1985). So, as well as isolating themselves from their feelings, as we discussed in Chapter 7, we see officers isolating themselves from people outside the law enforcement community, further fostering negative coping mechanisms. This isolation can become more pronounced the longer an officer serves. According to Violanti and Paton (1999), the law enforcement community pressures officers to conform, encouraging solidarity among its officers as a way of protecting the group from those outside the profession who are perceived as being unable to understand.

These officers begin to associate only with other officers (socializing, drinking, working out in gyms), and may even reside together in police officer-dominated neighbourhoods, losing contact with others outside the profession, until the only relationships available are with other police officers. This can continue as officers then begin to only trust the colleagues in their station, or on their shift. Police officers can easily become isolated from society, from the public, from the police organization, from fellow officers, and from their own families. As officers socialize only with other officers, so they become more isolated from the rest of society, only dealing with the trouble-making 5 per cent. This can then skew their views over time, and they can lose sight of the fact that it is only 5 per cent of society that is like this, because it is actually 95 per cent of the people the officers are likely to encounter.

We continue this exploration of isolation in Chapter 13, and develop it further, from isolation among police officers to isolation among leaders.

Case 5

Eyes Wide Open

Sergeant Eric Kellogg

In the late spring and early summer of 1995 I was a young police officer in one of the largest cities in Michigan. I was trying to make sure that I understood the job of being a police officer, of being a servant to the community, which is what I believe a modern-day police officer should be. I was receiving a great deal of input from my Field Training Officers (FTOs), the various old-school sergeants that I worked for, and the various tenured officers who had done it and seen it all.

While my FTOs and my sergeants should have had the greatest impact on me about how I did the job, in reality I found that the old-school officers initially had the greatest impact on how I did the job. They were always willing to impart their wealth of knowledge at some very inopportune times and in some very precarious and questionable officer safety moments. They always seemed to mean well, and their willingness to offer their wisdom was their way of acknowledging me as an individual worthy of occupying the job that had defined them for so long, a job to which they were likely to have possibly sacrificed their first marriage or their sobriety.

It was their version of positive reinforcement, and it was far better to receive the often off-color, negative, profanity-infused information than to be shunned and ignored. I took it and appreciated it for what it was—simply information. I likened it to my high school football days, when any attention from the coach was better than no attention; at least he acknowledged my existence, even if he was yelling at me.

Many of these old-school officers had joined the police force right after Vietnam, and carried with them the difficulties associated with that honorable and challenging experience. In addition, I recognized that when they started in this career field, it was considered more of a blue-collar type of career with little training. As a matter of fact, I recall many of those officers who were willing to share their knowledge with me say that they had received no field training, and had only ridden along with a senior officer for a night or two and then were on their own. I will say that those men who were able to learn the job were impressive, as they were able to maintain a level of competency through this wildly changing career. I was impressed with their commitment to a job they appeared to hate. These men were hard workers. For as much as they complained, they truly exemplified the old adage of "a good day's pay for a good day's work." As the son of a factory worker, that made me feel right at home.

That is not to say that all the old-school officers I came in contact with were the soured, hardened types. One of these old-school officers gave me the best piece of police advice I have ever received to this day, and it took me a bit to understand it. This is a piece of advice I share with every new recruit I get the opportunity to train. Now that I am a sergeant, I never miss the opportunity to pass on that piece of advice to newer officers.

This officer was an exceptionally humble man, not an FTO. However, I had the opportunity to ride with him as he functioned as my FTO for two days in my first week on the street. My assigned FTO had been injured early in the week and there were no other FTOs available. While he didn't volunteer, he was the only one who was not hostile during the shift briefing when the sergeant asked for someone to take me for the last two days of the week. In our first two hours together, I learned he was a man who had been a police officer for 33 years and had watched the ever-changing landscape of law enforcement. He had seen the writing on the wall and had obtained his criminal justice degree, emphasis in psychology, as a means to be the best officer he could be. He told me that he had no desire to pursue advancement. I think he would have made a great sergeant. He was a great leader who did not allow his peers to influence his principle-based leadership style. He simply listened and assessed what the person's needs were, and tried to meet those needs. He just wanted to serve the public in the way that best honored their needs. He noted that if they were not in need, we would not have been there with them; whether they called us, or our presence in their life at that time was divinely inspired, it mattered not. I noticed that while he was very different from the other old-school officers, they respected him and would often follow his lead while on a call, even if it was not the easiest way to handle the situation. He did what was right for the public that we were serving in each case.

I found that he was more proud of raising his family and of the loving relationship he had maintained with his wife for 36 years than being a police officer. He was a husband, a father, and a well-balanced person who was also a police officer, rather than being a police officer who was also a husband and a father.

In our final hour together before our weekend, he asked if I had any questions. I noted that I was impressed with his commitment to the public and his thoroughness in his duties. His response was cautionary, noting that I would soon start to feel the pull of wanting to make the big arrest and be part of the big incident. He also explained that I could start to feel the drudgery of the calls that were not "the big one." He explained that I *should* want to be part of those things as a young officer. However, he cautioned, my job was to serve the public and meet *their* needs, not my own desire to be part of the big arrest or incident.

He further noted that the big arrests would surely come, but that if I wanted to serve my own needs, I should seek to serve my need for balance, lest I become consumed by my job and fail to serve the public. He noted that many of the officers he has seen lose their lives while on duty were the "seven-year guys" who had turned "mean" because they were burnt out and missed the simple, obvious things. He summed this piece of advice up by saying, "No matter what you are doing, you are getting paid the same." He said this three times and asked me if I understood what he was saying, and I nodded my head dutifully in the affirmative, understanding the words but wondering what the hell that meant.

I was able to get through the FTO phase of my training rather quickly, and soon found myself on my own, feeling somewhat unprepared for the job of police officer in this racially charged city, complete with drugs, prostitution, a gang problem, and a large homeless population.

I was very excited to go to work every day and finally get comfortable with the job, and I will admit I liked the excitement. But I wanted to transform myself into the public servant I had pictured in my mind. I thought of this often on the way to work, and tried to understand what my teacher/mentor meant by his words of advice. However, the constant exposure to the old-school way of doing things set in rather quickly and threatened to rob me of my "gung-ho" attitude and work ethic that had stood me so well through my time in the military, college, and the police academy.

I was comfortable with the para-military way of life of police work. I had been in the service for ten years. After the service, I attended the University of Nebraska and achieved my BS in Criminal Justice. Ironically, as I was going to school I had no interest in becoming a police officer, and actually had a distaste for the idea. I had worked for seven years with troubled youth and their families, and was happily supervising a residential youth program.

I am embarrassed to admit this, but at about that same time the television show *Cops* became very popular, and I realized that police work was something that I felt I was well suited for and had a strong desire to do. I recognized that the de-escalation skills I had been practicing with the troubled youth and their families would be a great asset in police work. Sure enough, those skills have served me well, and my shift partners quickly recognized some of these skills, calling me over to their calls when they couldn't communicate with someone.

Yet I still struggled with the type of police officer I would be. It was very easy to simply fall into the same mold that the old-school officers came from and were perpetuating. However, I did not want to be the foul-mouthed angry police officer that would end a conversation with the public in a way that trivialized their needs and degraded the profession of police officer. But I found myself in just that position and frame of mind on one of the afternoons in this first late summer, early fall that I worked as a solo patrol officer.

It was the middle of my week, and I woke up that day in a funk. I was tired and somewhat angry about something I still to this day cannot identify. It was a typically warm and extremely humid day in Michigan, and we were privileged to see the sun this afternoon, as it had been raining for much of the previous week. I had been assigned to work Charlie sector, which at that time included the downtown park area where the homeless population congregated, waiting for the soup kitchen to open so they could get some dinner and then, with some luck, be able to get a bed for the night at one of the missions. These places filled up very quickly every night.

This proved to be an afternoon of firsts for me. It was the first time I had stopped one of our command staff for speeding, the first time I had really gotten my backside chewed since I was in basic training, the first time my wife of seven years and I had ever gotten into a real fight complete with yelling, it was the first time I had ever seen her cry about something I had said. It was the first time I had ever responded to a "dead on arrival" (DOA) call, *and* it was the first time I met Earl.

I responded to a street where I seemed to spend a lot of my time when working Charlie sector. I was the primary officer on what had initially been dispatched as a call to a homeless person who was unresponsive. I was assigned a cover car due to the unknowns associated with this type of call and the volatility of the location. Due to my being the new guy, I fully expected and welcomed the fact that I would be "taking the paper" (completing the reports) on whatever this call turned out to be. I initially called off the cover car, believing it to simply be one of our many homeless persons wasting our time again with some medical issue that could easily be addressed if he or she would just stop drinking and go home. I responded to the location of the downed person, and right away realized that this downed person was, in fact, one of our well-known semi-homeless females. Even in my somewhat naive state I was able to see that she had died. I checked for a pulse and confirmed what I already knew to be true.

As I think back, I am still struck by the fact that I was not really fazed by the sight of this dead woman. Upon recognizing what I had, I started getting on with my duties. My training kicked in, and I called for additional units and a supervisor as well as a medical unit. Once the responding officers started showing up, I asked that they set up a tape perimeter, and recall actually being excited that I was handling this type of call. However, my diligence lacked reverence for this person and her soul.

I continued on with my duties and went to visit with the supervisor who had arrived on-scene at about the same time as the medical unit. The medical unit went right to work, and having done this sort of thing many times, they were careful not to move the body too much, to preserve whatever evidence there might be if this turned out to be a homicide.

Given the location and the homeless population that existed in this area, every death was initially treated as homicide until the cause of death could be determined or foul play ruled out. That is not to say that most deaths are not investigated initially as homicides. However, in this location, the investigations were maximized. The Forensic Unit was called out, along with the detectives, and I thought to myself, "Yes, the big one!" I fully expected to work alongside the detectives until the case was resolved. However, that was not how the scenario went, and I was immediately assigned to monitor and record all those who entered or left the crime scene, a relatively low-level task. Ultimately, I was relieved by one of the old-school officers, who took over my duty so that I could do his, and I waded into the sea of homeless people in the small park that sat about 60 yards west of where the body was located, to find out if any of them had seen anything.

At the time I did not realize why the old-school officer had taken my spot and sent me to speak with the possible witnesses among the homeless people who were waiting to get a bed for the night. I went over with one of my peers, another new recruit, and we interviewed the group of homeless persons standing in the park. We knew most of them, or had seen them around while on patrol.

As we got closer to the group, I quickly realized why the officer had given me his spot, as the pungent smell of stale, cheap beer and extreme body odor mixed with just a hint of generic cigarettes hit me like the proverbial ton of bricks. I had smelled some unpleasant smells in my time, as I had worked on my wife's family farm when I was in college. Each day as I drove to the farm, I passed a feedlot and was struck by the smell, and drove much faster to get away from it. But this smell coming from this group of homeless people was considerably worse, and as I got closer, I realized that it was actually making me sick to my stomach. I think that my partner was starting to feel the same way, as we both came to the idea that we would set up away from the group and call them to us one at time.

I spoke with each of my respective witnesses, getting their story, asking them every question I could think of. Their response was mostly all the same — "I don't know anything," mixed with the occasional, "Officer, could you spare a dollar?" Even in my newness, I simply stopped acknowledging their pleas for change.

After I was done speaking with each of the individuals and had really gotten nothing more than the victim's name, I turned and started heading back towards the crime scene. As I walked in that direction, I observed a man in his fifties or sixties standing about 20 feet from where the crowd had been. He would look at me and then towards the ground, and then back at me. He was cursing a line of expletives that even the experienced officers and my military buddies would have admired. His comments were not directed towards me, or anybody for that matter. But I felt that it needed to be addressed because he might offend the peace of the other homeless persons in the area, so I approached him. I must say that as bad as the smell was coming from the group I had just talked to, this individual matched and surpassed the entire group.

He wore old, unlaced, black combat-style boots and what appeared to be gray dress suit pants with holes in both knees, which he tucked into the tops of the boots. There was some sort of sweatpant underneath the gray pants. He had on the matching suit coat to the pants, which was just as dirty as the pants, a black T-shirt with rust-colored suspenders and a red tie. To top off the ensemble, he wore a black, misshaped hat like a businessman in the 1950s might have worn.

As I approached him, I was careful to maintain my reactionary gap and told him to quiet down. I asked for identification. As if turning off a switch, he broke from his tirade of cursing at nobody in particular, his facial expression changed, and he stated that he did not have an ID. I was struck by the sudden change in his demeanor. He actually had a somewhat calm voice that came out just above a whisper. However, that was short-lived, and he returned to his tirade when one of the homeless people I had just spoken to came over to our location and told this person, "Shut the fuck up ... We are tired of listening to you."

The person who approached us explained that this was "Earl," and that the rest of the homeless population did not like him much because he was "crazy" and he "smells pretty bad." I didn't disagree with the message. However, I was struck by the irony, given the messenger, who had some strange characteristics of his own. Earl immediately began cursing again, and I thanked the individual for the information and told him to get back to the others.

While I stood there trying to figure out what to do, I started to listen to what he was saying, as I had previously just tuned out the words and had only heard the noise. In addition, he pointed to the crime scene, looked away, and then yelled. I realized that he might have information that would be beneficial to this case, and started down the arduous road of trying to calm him enough to get the information he might possess. I tried to talk in a calm voice, with no success, then I yelled at him in an effort to get him out of his hostile cyclical rant. Okay, as I think back, it might have been a bit out of frustration. I was sweating profusely, and felt that I had been "bumped out" of the investigation. I was standing near the homeless population, smelling them, and the longer I stayed, the more sick I was feeling.

However, even with my mounting displeasure with the situation, I still had a strong desire to get the job done and get the information that might help to explain what had happened to the victim. I recall at about that time looking around, hoping that one of my mentors might come and assist with this situation. However, I watched as they simply looked at me, snickered, and shook their heads. In hindsight, I had watched them avoid contact with our homeless population, and realized that they really had no additional information that would help me deal with this situation anyway. What they would more than likely tell me would be, "Leave the dirtbag," or "He's too fucked up to have anything we can use." Honestly, those were the thoughts going through my head.

However, as difficult as it was to stand in Earl's vicinity, I am a competitive person by nature, and I am not someone who likes to lose at anything. With some work, I was able to calm Earl somewhat. He now talked with gruffness about what his years on the street as a homeless person had taught him. At about the time he started to talk to me, I heard the loudest noise come from this man's stomach, and he began to wretch and vomit every ounce of fluid in his body. This was so disgusting. However, what made it even worse for me was the fact that he never stopped talking and telling me what he knew about the case we were investigating. He didn't bend over to throw up, as most would. He just simply stood there in a straight and erect posture and kept talking while vomiting the contents of his stomach out onto his chin, shirt, and the pavement.

I quickly stepped back and worked hard to keep my lunch down, and thanked Earl for his time. I will say that I did learn from Earl that the deceased sat there in the park early in the afternoon to eat her bag lunch that the mission had given her, and she had fallen asleep. I am sure it was a relatively short period of time while I listened to Earl. However, it felt like an eternity standing there, and I could not get away from him quick enough. I directed Earl to stay there, and I took over my original assignment. When the scene was finally cleared, it was confirmed by autopsy that she had died of natural causes—natural causes that I am sure were accelerated due to the stress of living as a homeless person.

As I got into my car to leave, I saw Earl still standing around, still engaged in the aggressive argument with nobody, just as he had been when I approached him initially. I stopped my police car an ample distance from Earl, recalling the disgusting details of our previous contact. And I directed, or maybe strongly suggested, that he get off the street for the night and get to the mission to get a bed. I asked if he needed me to call the mission for him. Earl's response was hostile, as expected, and when he told me to "Fuck off and leave me alone," I had to smile.

He then marched off, yelling about the fact that he had done what I had told him to and stayed there, and his sticking around to be a "good citizen" had forced him to miss dinner at the mission, and now he would be hungry all night. I remembered I did tell him to stay there, and I had completely forgotten to send him on his way. I felt bad. While my great old-school mentors would have said it was not a big deal and that he would survive, I still felt bad. It had only been a year or so earlier that I was working at a group home with kids and families who often did not have enough to eat. So I drove up to Earl and I gave him my sandwich from my lunch. I apologized for his missing dinner, and waited for a response. Earl took the sandwich and walked off, having paused in his argument with nobody long enough to grunt and ask what kind it was. To which he responded to himself out loud, "I guess it doesn't matter". He then continued his argument with nobody, and walked off.

It was strange, but I was actually embarrassed to have given him my sandwich. I was asked by one of the old-school officers later, "Was that dirtbag giving you shit?", noting that he saw me contact Earl as I was leaving. My response should have been, "No, I was giving him a sandwich because he was hungry." Instead, I made some stupid comment like, "I was just adjusting his attitude." The officer laughed and shook his head, acknowledging nonverbally that sometimes you have got to "put them in their place." As I said it, I hoped that I could justify it in my mind as having told the old-school officer the truth, as I hoped that I had adjusted Earl's attitude.

I can now thankfully say that was the first of many contacts with Earl. I do not say that to foreshadow any kind of wonderful, life-altering relationship with a homeless man that the movies so often want to portray. The truth is, Earl was the same person over the course of the next ten years as he was on the first day. He always smelled, and was always drunk. His vocabulary was mostly gruff, with the wonderful expletives I noted earlier, and was almost always vocally hostile.

I returned home that night, pleased for having fed Earl, or least I felt better that he would not go hungry. I found that my wife was still up, waiting for me to get home. We still had to speak about the argument that we had earlier. Truth be told, I was so happy that she had waited up so we could work it out, because there is no way I would have been able to sleep with that on my mind.

I am blessed to have a wonderful, caring wife who quite frankly won't put up with any shit from me. She will hold me accountable and stick to her guns.

I love and respect that about her. We worked out our disagreement, which was actually pretty simple because there actually had not been a disagreement. I was just being a jackass. We talked for a little while that night, and I shared with her my story of Earl and how it had made me feel good to do it. I recalled having a realization that night, in conversation with my wife, and I felt like this is what the modern-day police officer should do. I went to bed feeling happy and excited to return to work the next day.

Over the next several months, I distanced myself from the old-school mentality and just appreciated the fact that I had been chosen to shoulder the responsibilities of the modern-day police officer. I had several occasions to contact Earl. He seemed to always be in a place that made him a witness to the crime or incident that brought me to each scene. My wife had taken to packing my lunch for me, and after I shared my story of Earl with her, she started to pack two sandwiches each night, just in case I saw Earl. The extra sandwich always found its way to someone in need, and certainly Earl when I saw him.

Earl, like most who suffer from the various mental health challenges, had good days and bad. I was privileged to contact him on one of his few good days in the winter following my first contact with him. It was a viciously cold night, and the humidity seemed to chill through every layer of clothing I had on. On those types of nights, extra beds were set up all over the city's missions, to reduce the number of deaths from exposure. We were directed to try to get as many of the homeless into the shelters as possible. On this night, one of Earl's good nights, I found him in his normal place on the cement foundation under an overpass on one of the highways that intersects in our city. I gave him his sandwich, and spoke briefly with him about the fact that he should stay at the mission tonight. Earl was not his normal gruff self, arguing with nobody. I was actually speaking to a man who had a bit of a calm voice.

This was his moment of clarity, the only extended one I had seen Earl have. As I think about this, I wonder if it was more of a moment of clarity for me. Out of the blue, he said how much he had appreciated the way we—my wife, my partners, and I—had been treating him lately. He also asked if I wanted to see his ID. I had asked him each time to see his ID, and he had never been able to provide one. I always took his information and cleared him, and always found that there was a person by that name with that birthday matching his description. But I had never seen his identification.

Earl handed me his ID, and explained that he was going through his things today and had found it among some old pictures. As I was looking at his ID, I saw the name and birthday that he had been giving me all along. I was thankful that he had been honest each time.

I noticed the letters "MD" after his name. I initially confronted Earl about this, trying to establish whether this was a false ID or not. Earl immediately told me that it was not fake. He looked at the ground and put his hands in his pants pockets. I told Earl that his identification stated he was a medical doctor. Earl nodded his head and looked at the ground. As I think back, I still struggle with whether he was embarrassed when I found out or was simply being humble, as I believe the homeless are truly the most humble of us all.

Earl explained that he had been a doctor until approximately ten years or maybe fifteen years before I had initially contacted him. He explained that he was happily married, madly in love with his wife. They had two boys who had each gone to college, one to follow in his father's footsteps, and one to be a teacher. He smiled for the first time since I had met him, and he started to talk about his wife. He explained that he and his family lived in the area, and that approximately ten or maybe fifteen years earlier, his wife had passed from cancer. He said that no matter what they did, what treatment they pursued, she passed anyway as the cancer kept coming back.

Earl said, now with some shame, that he knew I probably thought poorly of him because he had abandoned his adult children. Earl explained that one day, about a year after she had died, he was on his way to work, and he stopped and picked up a bottle of vodka like he used to stop and get a bagel. He explained that from there, it was only a short slide to alcoholism. Within about two months of his starting to drink, he was living on the streets. As I was speaking to Earl, I started to notice the gruff Earl resurfacing, with short, angry comments being made to nobody. I tried to understand the transition from doctor to delusional homeless man, but Earl was slipping back into his street persona and was unable or unwilling to talk any further. I was able to convince Earl to go to the mission that night.

I had the honor of talking to Earl several times over the course of the next ten years while on patrol. On occasion, I would get to see the Earl of old for brief bursts of time, then as the memories became too painful, he would engage in the hostile argument he had been having with nobody since the first contact I had with him.

A short time later, I was given a great opportunity and assigned to the Special Response Team (SRT), which is a version of a SWAT (Special Weapons And Tactics) team. It was a full-time team, and I loved the intensity of the job. I enjoyed the privilege of working with the finest men and women I had ever worked with. They were well-balanced people who were also police officers. Their opinions of how the job should be done were very similar to my own. They showed me that the embarrassment I felt for having a warm spot in my heart for those like Earl is the act the true modern-day warrior.

I learned through my training that being kind or nice does not mean that you sacrifice officer safety. I was introduced to continuous, strenuous training fostering a winning attitude. Therefore, there was no need to posture and separate ourselves from maintaining a positive role model for the community we served. This attitude started with the commander of the team, flowing down to its newest members. The new members were quickly indoctrinated to adjust their attitude. If they couldn't figure it out, then the ridicule started.

It was recognized that fear is not a bad thing. However, when fear starts to take over the cognitive ability to control your response to whatever the situation is, then it becomes an issue. I also learned that it is much more productive to take an extra five minutes to calm an out-of-control person than to have to fight them. That extra five minutes is only five minutes, compared to the two or three hours of paperwork after "going hands on" with someone.

I worked with this group of people for approximately seven years. My wife continued to make Earl sandwiches. I was happy to get them to him any time I saw him. Often, my teammates would tell me over the radio or via the phone that they had contacted him at a location. When I was tied up, they would come and get the sandwich from my car and get it to him.

I loved working with these people, as they were the police officer I wanted to be. I worked each day to be good enough to work alongside them. They saw the people they dealt with for the people they were. They recognized that through their training they were in control and there was no need to dominate members of the public, but when the time came, they were prepared, able to handle any call. They took their time and addressed each issue as it came along, and did not rush to clear the call in the easiest way possible that entailed the least amount of work.

After about a year of working alongside these men and women, I recognized that the way they did the job with compassion and complete thoroughness was exactly what my original mentor was trying to communicate to me in his advice, "No matter what you are doing, you are getting paid the same." This statement was his mantra, his life thesis. Do your best in every situation, and take the time needed to do the job as completely as possible. Don't ignore the little things like honoring the person you are contacting. Attend to who they are and what their needs are. There are some needs that you will not be able to meet. But at the very least be conscious of them and acknowledge them. Treat them like people, and treat them as you would want to be treated. There is no sense in running to the next call if you don't have to when there is work to be done in front of you.

I am sad to say that the week when I was preparing to leave this department and move to another department in another part of the country, Earl went home to his wife. I say I am sad, but I am sure that Earl was not. He died of exposure during a week of extreme cold and very wet snow. I believe I might have been the last human contact Earl had in this life. I can't be sure, but I believe that I was.

I had moved to a job in investigations, and as I was driving a witness in a case to an interview in the late morning hours, I saw Earl. I drove under the overpass where he spent most of his time, and I could see someone was up on the foundation below the overpass. I walked up, and found Earl lying there, asleep and cold to the touch, with a somewhat calm look on his face. I was able to wake Earl, and his first comment was that he was with his wife, and I saw him smile a rare smile until he looked around and began his argument with nobody. He grabbed his stuff and walked away in a huff. I yelled after Earl that he should be at a shelter due the severity of the weather. He only looked back, waved me off, and kept walking. I was informed of his death the next morning. I was sad that this man who was once a happy family man in a helping profession had suffered such a difficult end to life. However, I get solace in the thought that this seemingly tormented man is at rest.

I recall this story often, and attribute this relationship to helping me to open my eyes to the officer I want to be: An officer that truly *serves* the community, whose own need to be part of "the big one" is secondary to the needs of those he or she is supposed to serve, to seeing each individual as a person who has a story. I recall this story often, so that I can be the best police officer the community can have, to honor Earl, my mentor, and the men and women of the SRT who helped me become the officer I feel we all should be.

Leader Reflection

- What stands out for you in this narrative regarding resilience?
- What elements of this narrative link to the aspects of resilience you are working with?
- What other elements of the narrative are important to you, and why?

11

Eyes Wide Open:
Analysis

Eric's narrative takes you through the beginning stages of his career as a new police officer, and his recognition of how he wanted to perform as a police officer, serving the public at the highest levels. There is current research in the police community which reports that most police officers believe in serving at their "highest levels" (Charles 2009; Smith and Charles 2010). Eric's story of Earl brings forth such vivid pictures of leadership themes, which is why we have chosen to focus on it. In addition, Eric's description of his mentor and the lessons he has learned about how to serve the public are paramount. The themes within his chapter illustrate many of the most important concepts for today's leaders – issues surrounding changing environments, listening skills, pursuing education to keep up with changes in the environment, ethical behaviours, and building relationships even when the individual is repulsive are all discussed from the perspective of today's leadership in any organization and culture.

Mentorship and Teaching

One of the first themes that emerges in the narrative is Eric's discussion of the "older officers" teaching him through example and demonstration. One of the most beautiful aspects within Eric's narrative is the discussion of how these older officers are such hard workers. His recognition of their quiet ability to demonstrate ethical behaviour reflects the importance of leaders leading by example, walking their talk in the workplace. Do you "walk your talk"?

While these officers talk in the narrative about the minimal training they have had to enable them to do their jobs, they work hard to learn the job as it changes drastically through the years. Eric's mentor recognized the increasing pace of police work, and chose to educate himself in order to increase skills, knowledge, and ability in his profession.

Attention and Approval

Eric talks about the older offers giving him attention, and says, "any attention is better than no attention". Chopra (2010) identifies research that demonstrates that if you work with someone who notices your strengths, your productivity and health remain at 99 per cent. If you work with someone who criticizes you, your productivity and health fall by 22 per cent. Finally, if you work with someone who ignores you, your productivity and health fall by 45 per cent. So it is better for you to be criticized than ignored – and there we were, thinking that some of our previous managers did not really care about us! Many of us, as leaders, have been brought up in our workplace with the understanding that "no news is good news". When we, as humans, want to be noticed and desire attention of some kind, we are left to wonder about how we are perceived and how are we performing. It is interesting to think that not talking with our peers, our families, and our employees may be hazardous to our health.

We all want to feel we are liked and appreciated for what we do and who we are. However, some can feel an excessive need for approval, and so spend large amounts of time and energy seeking it. This is unhelpful, stressful, and can drain their resilience. As Green and Humphrey (2012: 61) identify, feeling this need for approval can make it difficult and stressful to do things like maintaining boundaries, managing time and workload, and achieving a balance between work and outside life, because the person is constantly thinking about what they should do so they can gain approval from a significant person, rather than doing what is best or necessary. Achieving balance will always involve saying "no" to someone. Maintaining boundaries, managing time and workload, and achieving a work–life balance are key aspects for leaders, so it may be worth considering this issue of approval for a moment. Do you feel it necessary to seek approval from someone in your work or home life? If so, why is this, and what impact does it have on you and your resilience? What about people who work for you? Can you identify any who are constantly seeking your approval? If so, why might they be doing this, and what impact is it having on you, them, and their work? How might you be able to assist them to move forward on this issue?

Ethics and Values

Eric discusses how his most memorable mentor gave him the best piece of advice he has ever received. He has kept these powerful words near his heart each day he serves. What is interesting about Eric's mentor is how brief their encounter was, yet how powerful. We, as leaders, must remain cognizant of the fact that seemingly insignificant moments in our lives may bring the most impressionable concepts to those around us.

The informal leaders in Eric's career demonstrate the importance of recognizing that we need to get the job done, and it is up to us. Their ethical nature shines through as they work hard each and every day. Today, there are many of us wondering where this ethical nature or values system begins, and where it has gone. It appears to have become less important today in our workplaces. As leaders, how do we instil these values back into our workplaces? If the ethics and values are there, how do we maintain and nurture them? Perhaps it is as simple as doing the right thing even when no one is looking. Maybe these informal leaders behaving ethically, regardless of popular opinion, is the best.

Eric's mentor had a tremendous effected on Eric's values. Eric describes a man who is not influenced by others around him. "He does what is right for the public," disregarding dissenting opinion. As leaders, maintaining our resilience through doing what is right versus what is popular lessens the stress of decisions (Travis 2009).

In Charles' (2005) research, several police officers expressed the importance of ethics and values. One said:

> *I can't imagine my being a police officer without having them [morals]. It's a frightening thought to me. If I had no moral compass, that thought of being in this position and doing this job is terrifying. I wanted to be a good cop. I needed that moral compass and I needed that grounding. You know what the right thing to do is. The answer's there. That is 99% of this job.*
> *(Charles 2005: 108)*

Another police officer reflected on the importance of spiritual integrity:

> *I think the most important thing you bring to the job is your ethics and your character. I just think it's in your heart and you've got to have a moral compass that just always points in the right direction no matter*

> *how bad the seas are around you. The compass has got to be always true*
> *and you either have it or you don't. You've got to dedicate yourself to it*
> *and you've got to have sound moral principles.*
>
> (Charles 2005: 108)

Another officer believed in the importance of spirituality and morality for police work:

> *Some people are into that uniform and that power thing and if you don't*
> *have your spirituality and morality, you kind of go the fast road because*
> *it's so easy. We have a lot of crime and deal with a lot of bad folks. If*
> *you're not a Christian or if you don't have something grounding you,*
> *you can get lost in it, kind of like a relative morality.*
>
> (Charles 2005: 108)

Eric's mentor describes being "balanced" in his position, of recognizing what is important in his life, and understanding that he is first a person, then a family man, and finally a cop. He finds importance in all areas of his life, but is balanced, and does not give the job more importance and definition of his person than necessary. Eric describes his mentor's piece of advice as critical to his own development. Yet this advice was given in the final hour of their working together, when his mentor said to him, "No matter what you are doing, you are getting paid the same."

When looking at our behaviour, our ability to balance our lives is an example of being ethical in our lives. To overburden our families with our work, never taking time to "be" with them, may be just as unethical as someone who shirks their duty, calling in sick when not, being dishonest, and failing to work diligently. Being present in our own lives offers a living example for others to follow.

This statement from Eric's mentor is so powerful, and yet so simple. However, it is intriguing to consider how this statement can be abused in various situations. For example, the scenario here is for Eric to do his best and serve the needs of the populace. What happens, though, if another individual finds this an appropriate way to avoid doing their best because "I'm getting paid the same"? It is imperative that individuals are ethical and have values that ground them to do justice to the advice. The importance of the ethical nature and doing the right thing even when no one is watching is critical.

The advice from Eric's mentor also reflects the importance of doing whatever task is in front of you, and doing it to the best of your ability. However, these words also illustrate the importance of *any* task: not always looking for the big deal or the biggest arrest, the next promotion, or the largest acquisition, but rather, how can you best serve this situation in front of you? As leaders, we often find ourselves in very competitive roles. It is one of the reasons why we are leaders. What we so often forget is to be cognizant of why we are competing. Is this next step good for our own growth and that of our families? Can we compete for that next position with integrity, instead of aggression or anger? So where does this ethical nature or values-based personhood come from, and how do we nurture it in ourselves and others?

Perhaps, as leaders, we need to remember how to nurture this value-based personhood in order to maintain our resilience. Eric talks about the strong desire to transform into an excellent public servant. How do we support someone's desire to be the best at their job? Can we find a solution to encourage someone, rather than being discouraging and fostering distrust, lack of integrity, and dishonesty?

Eric talks about how easy the temptation is to turn into one of the "older officers" who are "burned out" and shouting expletives, As we explored a little in Chapter 9, it is easy to see how this happens in the police community; those are the officers who receive the most attention from their peers, the public, and their administration. Albeit negatively, they get noticed. Attention-seeking like this can be a result of traumatic experiences the person is still holding within their body and mind, according to Rees and Smith (2008). So maybe we should take time to notice what our peers or employees are doing and saying, to listen and talk to them, and to support them more.

Eric's description of meeting Earl places us right in the situation with him. The smells of the homeless people, the picture of Earl vomiting on himself, and the expletives shared loudly by the vagrant population are very vivid to the reader. While, as leaders, we may not be in contact with this precise type of repulsive behaviour, there may be plenty of opportunity to address or deal with employees or customers who are repulsive in their behaviour. We may have to address situations where dishonesty or unethical or bullying behaviour slaps us in the face. Eric's personal reflection on how he was dealing with people of this type as "my diligence lacked reverence for this person and her soul" is breathtaking. He is able to clearly state that there must be compassion and listening to what the needs of the person in front of us are. If we fail to listen, then we may lose the chance to hear the message that may lead us to the next right thing. Or we may miss a seemingly insignificant moment that may become a momentous one for us or those we encounter.

He describes being somewhat disappointed in being assigned a "lower-level task" rather than the glory job of an investigator. He clearly recognizes his ego and his desire to be involved in the "next big thing". Eric inspires us with the recognition of what his mentor has schooled him on – to remember, "No matter what you are doing, you are getting paid the same." It is easy for us, as leaders in organizations, to let our egos or our competitiveness get the best of us, leading us astray from what is truly important. Perhaps we might ask more often: "What is the best way I may serve the needs of those directly in front of me?"

Our competitive nature is what has driven us to become leaders, but the message here is far deeper. We must remain cognizant to staying balanced, not letting our ego consume us, and must remain compassionate to those in front of us. We can push our families behind us when they need us, thinking we are most important to our profession. Once successful in our profession, we can forget what it is that called us to our work. We forget the "why" about our job, and seek the next big thing, completely missing the gifts that lie directly at our feet, should we choose to look.

Listening and Building Relationships

Learning to listen fully is a difficult task for most of us. Yet it is one of our most important responsibilities. As leaders in our organizations and community, we need to provide open communication with our peers, our employees, our families, and our communities. Often, we are the spokesperson when we should be the audience. When we fail to listen, some of the most beautiful gifts pass us by, such as seeing the hidden messages from a homeless man with incredible knowledge, who happens to be intoxicated.

Eric describes the importance of listening to someone who probably has not been heard in years. He tells us that Earl smells, shouts expletives, and finally vomits all over himself while he's talking. Yet Eric listens as Earl tells him about the woman who died, which is what brought him to the medical scene. Certainly, Earl's appearance might give Eric cause to be dismissive of him. Instead, he listens. He also describes how his peers are dismissive of Eric and his interaction with Earl. Eric's behaviour is the beginning of his "doing the right thing" when it is not a popular course of action – truly a tremendous step forward in his progress as a good police officer and a human being. The moment is insignificant in itself, yet in the larger scheme, it is the beginning of a strange and wondrous relationship between two unlikely people: a homeless drunk and a young cop. Sometimes our greatest teachers are the most unusual characters.

Leaders in today's world are tasked with having to deal with constantly increasing changes in information. There is a demand to gather more and more data, make changes based on the information, produce efforts with fewer personnel and less finances, and increase efficiency and effectiveness. However, sometimes we forget to stop and just listen: listen to ourselves or our loved ones, listen to those in front of us, and listen to the needs of others. We push forward instead of stopping … to just listen.

Once Eric is finished at the scene, he describes Earl just standing around, shouting expletives at no one. When Eric tells him to move on, Earl reminds Eric that he was told to stay there and he complied, even in his mental state. However, Earl has now missed his opportunity to eat for the day. Eric could have "dismissed" Earl and told him to leave and not cared about whether he ate for the day. Instead, Eric makes one of the grandest gestures in his abilities as a leader and a human being. He gives Earl his own sandwich out of his lunch. The ability to look at ourselves and our imperfections and ask forgiveness is monumental, and goes so far.

This is another area where some leaders may find themselves on difficult terrain. It takes true leadership to be able to look at one's mistakes and correct them. There is such power in our acknowledgement of our frailties and our overcoming the mistakes we have made. Eric's acceptance of his errors and his rectification of those errors have led him into this unusual friendship with Earl. There is acceptance of Earl's condition, and recognition of Eric's limitations in what he can do for Earl.

Eric chooses to share his experience with his wife upon his return from work that night. He recognizes his "mistakes" in the argument he had with his wife before work and wants to resolve any issues with her. Research in the police culture shows us that most police officers tend to compartmentalize their job and separate it from their families (Violanti and Paton 1999). Unfortunately, this behaviour can further isolate officers from their families, thereby distancing them and their feelings, and the valuable support mechanism they can provide.

This behaviour can lead to distrust and cynicism in police officers, as well as an "us versus them" mentality (Gilmartin 2002). Eric's choice to communicate his work stories provides common ground for both husband and wife to "share" in each other's lives. Our workplaces require much of our time and focus, so it is imperative to disclose what we can to our families so that there is "shared" understanding and recognition of the work we do.

Do you share what you have been doing with your partner and family? If not, what prevents this? If you do, what benefits do you notice from doing this?

Upon Eric sharing the story of Earl with his wife, she collaborates with him and begins to pack lunches for Earl as well. As Eric works in this sector, he learns more about his street friend, accepting the limitations of Earl and offering what he can. He recognizes that Earl is limited in his responses, and that Eric is limited in what he can offer to Earl. There is no payoff for Eric as he builds this relationship with Earl. This relationship does not give him the next promotion or an advancement of salary. He is paid the same for this work as another cop is for being rude and aggressive with the public and homeless. However, he is becoming the police officer he wants to be, the best public servant he can be. What has made the difference, do you think? How can we help each other to grow compassionately in our professions without stepping on one another?

On one sane night, Earl tells Eric how much he appreciates the kindness from Eric and his peers. Eric has joined a team that shares the same belief system. They train to make the best decisions, and do not feel a need to posture or push themselves on another human being. They believe in listening compassionately, training to be at their best, and being fully present each day at work. Earl acknowledges that their treatment of him has offered him peace in such a stressful life on the streets. Earl then discloses more information about himself. He turns his life inside out, and tells Eric what it was that brought him to this state of homelessness. The losing of his beloved wife knocked him out of balance, turning him to alcohol, and then the streets. It was such an easy and very quick transition for one human being, and illustrates very powerfully how much we all need our support networks, as we explored in Chapter 1.

Conclusion

The larger lesson offered to Eric was a message of balance. Because Eric paid attention to all the messages, he was able to maintain his balance as he learned his new career and as he grew up in the police community. Eric found like-minded peers who embodied the same values and ethics and made his job more meaningful. Because of that, Earl could share his life with another person prior to his death. It may have been the only or last time that Earl could or would have shared that lesson.

The concept of leadership Eric describes comes from his commander and spreads out to the officers. There is a winning attitude, where the team trains constantly and strenuously to develop mind and body. There is no need to posture or impose oneself on another. The team members develop their own resilience and maintain it for each other when times are difficult. Eric gives us the example of his team letting him know where Earl is so that he can get him that nightly sandwich. This is a great example of how we, as leaders, can be most effective and efficient for our people, how important it is to walk our talk.

As leaders, maybe what we must work toward is building our own resilient mind, body, and spirit. Once the concept is ingrained, then we can look to build the team with others who are of the same mind. Those who choose not to comply will fade out. The team then creates the furtherance of the resilience of its workplace.

This statement from such a wise man – "No matter what you are doing, you are getting paid the same" – is very powerful. Do your best in every situation, and take the time needed to get the job done as completely as possible. Don't ignore the little things, like honouring the person in front of you. Attend to who they are and what their needs are. You won't be able to meet all their needs, but at the very least be conscious of them and acknowledge them.

When Eric learns of Earl's death, he hears his mentor's words again and knows he could not have met all of Earl's needs. He had attempted to get Earl in from the cold, but also knew that Earl was his own person with the ability to make his own decisions, even those that led him to the end of his life.

What is most beautiful about this chapter and its story is the humility of its author as Eric brings what he has learned to life for the readers. It is the insignificant moments that create such beauty and powerful messages. It is these moments that teach us, lead us to the next great thing, and allow us to recognize the miracles in front of us as we grow as human beings and leaders.

Case 6

12

Leadership in Crisis

Sir Peter Fahy

Police leadership throws you into many challenging situations, many of which test your personal limits, and many of which create ethical dilemmas. There are often many conflicting pressures, tight timescales, and a mixture of short-term imperatives and long-term considerations. You are aware that your decisions and actions will be subject to much scrutiny and questioning by a range of different interests. They may be picked over in the cold light of day many years after, and with the great benefit of hindsight, or a very different mindset. There are often conflicts between what is the right thing to do for an individual and what may be the wider organizational interest. You may be under pressure to avoid admitting liability, to preserve the reputation of the organization, or to establish or maintain a principle.

The best way through this is to be really clear about your own values and your own sense of vocation. Why are you in the public service, what drives you, what's important to you? From this, you can be clear about your own line in the sand – to put it bluntly, what would you resign over, what would cause you to make a complaint about a colleague or your boss? It is also important to know the law and the particular rules about your own position. If you are clear and confident about this, you are in a better position to recognize when you or someone else is going wrong.

You need to give yourself the time to reflect on this, to take time out of the hurly-burly to step back and give yourself some space. For me as a Christian, this comes from daily prayer and an hour spent in church every Sunday, but others will have their own time and techniques to reflect on whether they are remaining true to themselves or not. I think it is also important, no matter how high you are in the corporate world, that you constantly return to the front line of your organization and experience the reality for your own staff and for the public. This reminds you what is the core mission of your organization, and will also remind you that you have a tremendous workforce trying to do its best. It reinforces that it is the public's experience of your service that matters most, and it helps to close the gap between what you think is happening and the reality of service delivery.

I have dealt with many high-profile cases during my service when you suddenly find yourself and your organization under great public scrutiny and at the top of the headlines. The lesson I have learnt is that the stories of success are never as good as they first seem, and the stories of failure are never quite as bad. I try to keep a sense of balance and remain stoical. Then it's about building the right support structure around you. The best thing you can do as a leader in a crisis is to sort out who is responsible for what, and ensure they have the resources they need to do the job you are asking them to do. When situations go wrong, it is often because accountabilities are blurred or confused. Once you have clarified this, you need to get the right balance between letting them get on with it and exercising scrutiny over what they are doing and being there as a sounding board.

Personal reliance is also strengthened by the quality of advice and challenge you are receiving. Certainly, policing has always been improved by greater accountability and openness. Therefore, actively encouraging feedback and challenge will help you survive, and ultimately succeed. Different situations need different approaches, but bringing in independent community members, being as open as possible with the press, and building links with families and victims involved may be painful at first, but will pay dividends.

You need to keep a sense of perspective in the eye of a storm. For me, getting home to my family and being reminded that Greater Manchester Police is not the most important thing in the world helps prick any balloon of self-importance or pomposity I may have created around me. Close friends and colleagues are an enormous support if you give them the space to talk to you.

Your instincts are often right. When things have not gone well, I have often reflected that there was a small voice telling me at an early stage that this did not feel right. If you hear that voice, listen to it, even if it will make you unpopular and you end up disagreeing with some of your key staff.

One of the most difficult dilemmas is the balance between what might be the organizational need and what might be the interests of an individual member of staff or group of staff. When do you need to show flexibility and make an exception, and when is it important to set a principle or follow an established policy? Sometimes in trying to be fair to a wider group of staff, you end up creating disadvantage for individuals. This is never easy. You need to test the principle and your own thinking and be clear about the logic you are following. Be careful and watchful, however: some will want organizational tidiness, and showing flexibility and looking at individual circumstances may seem harder work than maintaining a common line, but it may be the right thing to do.

I don't see that any of this will get any easier. The public spotlight and level of scrutiny will only grow. The dilemmas to be faced will only become more complex. Leaders will need to be more transparent in their decision-making and display integrity and authenticity in all aspects of their personal conduct. They will be wise to establish means of external scrutiny and challenge where they can play out ethical dilemmas. They will need to be even more assured of their own values and the principles they work to. They will want to create healthy organizations where staff can raise concerns and challenge inappropriate behaviour or practices which go against the public interest. This is easier said than done. Many of the decisions you are faced with are not straightforward, and there may be arguments on both sides or on many sides. The drive to find individuals accountable when things go wrong is understandable and necessary when individual failings have brought about a situation. Individuals often work in complex systems, however, and there is seldom just one cause. Too much hindsight and a preponderance of what may appear as scapegoating rather than learning lessons may work against the public interest in the long term, and certainly makes leadership even harder.

Leadership Reflection

- What stands out for you in this narrative regarding resilience?
- What elements of this narrative link to the aspects of resilience you are working with?
- What other elements of the narrative are important to you, and why?

13

Leadership in Crisis: Analysis

Introduction

This narrative brings both a leadership and a police officer perspective, coming as it does from the leader of Greater Manchester Police (GMP), one of the largest provincial police forces in England and Wales. GMP's budget is over £560 million per annum, and it employs over 7,500 police officers, nearly 700 special constables, and 200 volunteers. Alongside these are over 4,000 police staff who provide professional support to frontline policing. During the last financial year, GMP recorded more than 200,000 crimes and dealt with more than 95,000 detainees at its custody sites. The force takes around 1,400 emergency calls and deals with about 2,500 incidents every day.[1]

Sir Peter's narrative provides many powerful insights which stand in their own right and need no further analysis. The narrative also reinforces many of the points that have been raised in previous chapters, highlighting the importance of: vocation and finding larger purpose and meaning; finding time to be; reflection; some form of spiritual practice; listening to your inner voice; family, close friends, and colleagues; values-based decision-making, and holistic approaches to leadership. The number of areas that reinforce discussions in previous chapters of this book is particularly interesting and significant, as Sir Peter had not seen these chapters prior to writing his narrative.

---

1   Figures as of March 2012.

Leadership Isolation

In Chapter 9 we explored the issues of isolation for police officers. This is an important factor that needs to be considered within policing. The feeling of isolation can also be experienced in leadership roles, particularly as you reach more senior positions. Employees can seem to be afraid of talking to you, or of telling you anything but positives and good news. It can also be difficult as a leader to discuss with others the sensitive information you have about the organization. In the narrative, Sir Peter identifies that he feels that self-reliance can be strengthened by the quality of advice and challenge you are receiving, and he suggests that actively encouraging feedback and challenge will help you survive, and ultimately succeed.

Millett (2012) reports:

> *The intensity of the CEO's job, coupled with the scarcity of peers to confide in, creates potentially dangerous feelings of isolation among chief executives. Fifty percent of all CEOs report experiencing loneliness in the role, and of this group, 61% believe that the isolation hinders their performance. First-time CEOs are particularly susceptible to this isolation, with nearly 70% of those who experience loneliness saying it negatively affects their ability to do their jobs. Nearly half of all CEOs estimate that most other leaders experience similar feelings of loneliness.*

This quotation specifically concerns CEOs, but we would argue that it applies to many other leadership roles as well. Sutton (2009) also suggests that leaders can become more self-absorbed and less attuned to others' perspectives, and so need outside information more, just at the time when they are becoming more isolated. This can then lead to the larger problem of poor decision-making that we discussed in Chapter 9, due to a lack of information, or accurate information.

Do you feel isolated in your role as a leader? If so, what specific things do you notice, and what effects do these have on you? What might you be able to do to feel less isolated? Do you think others you work with or lead feel the same way as you? If they feel isolated, what might you be able to do to enable others to feel less isolated?

We wonder also about feelings of isolation among leaders within the police service. Do they experience a dual difficulty here in feeling the isolation we have identified as a result of being a police officer as well as the isolation we have highlighted from being a leader? How many other examples of dual difficulties can you identify – for example, discrimination as a result of being a woman police officer, from being a person who is black and has a disability? What are the implications of these dual pressures? We will explore a little more of this in Chapter 15.

Sir Peter highlights the enormous support that can be provided by family, close friends, and colleagues – "if you give them the space to talk to you". Do you give your family, friends, and colleagues the space to talk to you? How do you actually do this? Do they know this?

The impact of feeling really connected to, and being able to talk openly with, other human beings can be very powerful. Woodham (1995: 114) identifies the benefits that talking through problems can have. There is a common saying, "A trouble shared is a trouble halved," and this highlights the benefits that can result from talking through problems and connecting with others. In Ron's narrative in Chapter 8, we saw a practical example of how quickly and easily this was done, and what a major impact it had on Ron's life. Whilst we can only speculate, it seems likely that it may well have had a similar impact on the other people's lives too.

As a leader, how are you able to connect with other people? What enables you to do this, what gets in your way, and do you want to have closer connections with others? If you feel you may be able to develop these connections more, what impact would making a more positive connection with your employees have on you, the employees, their families, the organization, the planet, and both their and your own resilience?

Values

We have talked in previous chapters about the importance of meaning, purpose, and sense of vocation for building resilience that Sir Peter discusses in his narrative. Linked to these, this narrative also highlights the importance of values, and being really clear about your own values.

At their simplest, our personal values reflect what is important to us. Rokeach (1979: 48) suggests values are "socially shared conceptions of the desirable", and that we employ values as standards to guide us and help us decide what is and is not worth arguing about – what you would "resign over, what would cause you to make a complaint about a colleague or your boss", in Sir Peter's words.

Schwartz (2006: 1) suggests that some of the main features of the conception of basic values that are implicit in the writings of many theorists and researchers are as follows:

- Values are beliefs. But they are beliefs tied inextricably to emotion, not objective, cold ideas.

- Values are a motivational construct. They refer to the desirable goals people strive to attain.

- Values transcend specific actions and situations. They are abstract goals. The abstract nature of values distinguishes them from concepts like norms and attitudes, which usually refer to specific actions, objects, or situations.

- Values guide the selection or evaluation of actions, policies, people, and events. That is, values serve as standards or criteria.

- Values are ordered by importance relative to one another. People's values form an ordered system of value priorities that characterize them as individuals. This hierarchical feature of values also distinguishes them from norms and attitudes.

According to Barrett (2006: 159), values can be positive or potentially limiting. For example, honesty, trust, and accountability are positive values, whereas blame, revenge, and manipulation are potentially limiting. Positive values are known as virtues. Barrett (2006: 161) argues that these positive values emanate from the soul, and the limiting ones emanate from the conscious or subconscious fear-based beliefs of the ego. The behaviours associated with potentially limiting values support the ego in meeting its needs. Blame is seen by the ego as a way of avoiding humiliation. Revenge is seen by the ego as a way of getting even. Manipulation is seen by the ego as way of manoeuvring to get its needs met. Barrett (2006: 163) argues that personal mastery involves letting go of the ego's limiting values, and replacing them with the values (virtues) of the soul.

In the organizational context Barrett (2003: 356) argues that for organizations to achieve long-term success, they needed to demonstrate a strong alignment between personal values of employees and the values of the organization. Barrett argues, from his experience of mapping the values of more than 2,000 private and public sector institutions over the past ten years in more than sixty countries, that values-driven organizations are the most successful ones on the planet. He argues that the reasons for this are as follows:

- Values and behaviours drive culture.

- Culture drives employee fulfilment.

- Employee fulfilment drives customer satisfaction.

- Customer satisfaction drives shareholder value.

We explored values-based decision-making in Chapter 9, and Barrett (2006) argues that the reasons this values-based decision-making is important at this time in our human history are as follows:

- Values allow us to transcend our ethnic/cultural beliefs and structures by uniting us around shared basic human principles. He argues that in human group cultures, values unite, but beliefs separate. If this is true, then values-based decision-making can assist the development of democracy around the world.

- Values-based decision-making allows us to throw away our rulebooks. When a group of people espouse an agreed set of values and understand which behaviours support those values, then you no longer need to rely on bureaucratic procedures setting out what people should or should not do in specific situations. All the rules reduce to one – live the values. People can work out for themselves what they need to do, and in so doing become responsible and accountable for their behaviours.

All this serves to re-emphasize the importance of personal values and aligning personal and organizational values. If you have not had the opportunity for a while to consider the values that are important to you, a useful exercise to enable you to do this is provided by Roberts (2012).

Bravery

According to Trungpa (2009: 3), many approaches to spirituality and life in general are influenced by cowardice. If you are afraid of seeing yourself, you may use spirituality or religion as a way of looking at yourself without seeing anything about yourself at all. Bravery, according to Trungpa (2009), is about overcoming both fear and cowardice, and is about honesty.

In Sir Peter's narrative, we see many aspects of bravery being demonstrated – through high-profile cases and during the "eye of the storm". As the leader of an organization such as the police, particularly in the UK, we also feel Sir Peter is demonstrating this bravery in the openness and honesty with which he shares with us his views and personal beliefs. It is refreshingly liberating to hear talk of vocation, the importance of close friends and family, honesty, integrity, authenticity, values, and spiritual beliefs and practices.

Within our work and research, we see many aspects of bravery being demonstrated by police officers every day. As another example, Walsh (2008), who was on duty as a police officer when the twin towers were attacked on 9/11, talks of seeing many thousands of people running away from the falling towers, trying to escape, while police officers and firefighters were running the opposite way – towards the falling buildings – to try to help people. What is it that enables these officers and firefighters to do this?

The Future

Sir Peter suggests that the challenges for leaders and police officers are unlikely to get any easier in the future. He also offers a number of powerful points that may be of assistance in order to build resilience to be able to cope with increasing challenges, complexity, and sharper scrutiny:

- Leaders will need to be more transparent in their decision-making and display integrity and authenticity in all aspects of their personal conduct.

- They will need to be even more assured of their own values and the principles they work to.

- They need to establish means of external scrutiny and challenge so that they can play out ethical dilemmas.

- They need to create healthy organizations where staff can raise concerns and challenge inappropriate behaviour or practices.

As identified in the narrative, this is hard though, and requires bravery and resilience, but it does challenge many of the current poor leadership practices which Rayment and Smith (2011) identify as "misleadership".

Case 7

14

Policing for Peace in Northern Ireland – the Four Voices

Tim Meaklim

Joining the Royal Ulster Constabulary (RUC) as a teenager at the start of the 1980s was an exciting but very dangerous thing. Street protests, murders, and explosions were the normal expectations for society in Northern Ireland, and the police force was there to detect, contain, and prevent acts of violence, investigate crime, and provide as normal a policing service as could be expected. Unfortunately, the makeup of the RUC along with the inequalities and sectarian hatred that existed at that time meant that the police were seen as partisan, a tool of the United Kingdom, and more crucially, the Protestant Unionists in Northern Ireland.

But as a young man I didn't care about politics; I believed that I was doing something to help all society in a particularly difficult time. I had left school, but had not identified a clear career path. I knew that I wanted to do something that involved working with people. My grandfather had been a member of the RUC, as had some of my great-uncles; at the time it seemed almost natural to apply to join the police. Unlike my parents, I did not believe that I was at risk. Other people died or were injured, but not me. This was the first of my voices. This voice was a personal message telling me that I should join the police and make a difference. This voice brought an excitement and satisfaction about doing something positive for the community. It also helped me to mitigate the possible risks of being a police officer in Northern Ireland. However, I did understand the dangers, and routinely carried a revolver on and off duty. I ensured I didn't let people know what my job was, and I took great care in planning any journeys I took. I was aware that as a police officer I was a prime target. Interpol statistics indicated that Northern Ireland was at the time the most dangerous place in the world to be a police officer – more than twice as risky as serving in El Salvador, the next most hazardous location (River Path Associates 2002). Although there were many occasions I felt fear in the situations I was working and living in, this was countered by a voice in my head telling me that I was doing a necessary job and that terrorism could not be allowed to win.

In those early years I worked in a rural area, then a city, and then in a mobile support unit with a key responsibility for public order and counter-terrorist duties. During this period I was fortunate to meet and fall in love with my wife. She was from a different religious and community background to my own, which made our relationship complex and not universally accepted. The behaviour of our respective churches probably pushed us away from organized religions. How could "Christians" be so openly hostile towards one another? As a result, we decided to move to England after our marriage. This decision was very difficult, as we had to leave behind our families and loved ones; however, we felt we needed the opportunity to start our married life without the pressures of the troubles and the conflicts between our churches. I joined a county police service, while my wife finished off her studies before starting work. My understanding of normal policing concepts and good practices accelerated as I had time to engage with real policing issues without the challenges of sectarian violence. After the birth of our first child, we were faced with a dilemma: either to stay in England, but away from our families, or return to Northern Ireland with all of its challenges, but with the comfort of our families. In the end the decision was not difficult – we needed to be at home, and we returned to Northern Ireland and I rejoined the RUC. It was a strange feeling moving back. In many ways I was more experienced in policing, but I had to re-learn the skills of protecting not only myself, but for the first time thinking about the safety of my wife and child. It was not as simple as when I had first joined the RUC, and I was much more acutely aware of the dangers around me, both on and off duty. Perhaps I should have considered another job, but I was part of the policing family, and the voice still provided me with a desire to make a difference. Interestingly, my daughter was 13 years old before I first told her I was a police officer. It was easier to be a "civil servant" than to allow your true employment to be known in your neighbourhood.

In the period I had been away from the violence, the threat to members of the police force was higher than previously due to greater sophistication in weapons and explosive devices. While I had been away, a number of colleagues I had known had been killed or seriously injured. Deaths of those who were close to you were always harder to deal with than those you did not know. It was not as easy to disconnect the emotion.

I attended training to prepare me for dealing with possible gun or explosive attacks. I can still vividly remember one particular training event, part of which consisted of a mock terrorist attack on a police patrol. During the training practice, firearm rounds and practice explosives were used in a confined space, and as a result I lost 40 per cent of the hearing in both my ears. In many ways the event was not memorable in itself, as I received no other injuries and didn't properly recognize the injury at first, just the buzzing noise that lasted for a few hours. But even so, every detail of the day is still vivid in my mind.

The loss of hearing impacted on both my private life and my work life. Visits to both my own doctor and Hearing Specialist and a review by the Occupational Health Department of the RUC confirmed that my hearing loss was permanent. In reality, the injury had resulted in a loss of hearing equivalent to thirty years of ageing. I was informed that I was no longer medically fit to undertake operational roles which had the label "Non-Operational Officer".

As a relatively young man, my first reaction was that this could not be happening to me; I was a police officer, and I knew nothing else, my whole career to date had been spent carrying out operational duties. I now found myself in a lonely place, meeting with an Inspector in the Human Resources Department. I was worried about my future, and about having a job to support my wife and young family (my second child, a boy, had been born a few weeks before the training incident).

It is an interesting aspect of the human psyche that most of the things that go on around us take place without our ability to recall them. Scientists state that extreme emotional memories activate a process that ups the intensity of long-term memories in the same way that the volume control on a radio increases. Studies have shown that emotionally arousing events cause stress-related hormones such as adrenaline to be released by the brain, which impacts upon emotional learning and memory. The memories of my meetings connected to my hearing loss and my work have remained very intense, and have kept returning to me throughout my career. These, along with other emotional memories from work, have had a major impact on my behaviours.

I remember vividly the Human Resource Inspector's first question to me was, "Do you want to be medically discharged?" This question hit me like a train, I was in total disorientation, I felt fear for my future. It had never entered my mind that I might lose my job. For the first time I began to think that my time in policing was going to end soon. Despite the fact that I knew that I was intelligent, hard-working, loyal, and had potential, in those few words by that Inspector I now only saw limitations. Of course, if I had been medically retired I would have received a pension and financial compensation, but that is not what I wanted. I knew that the organization had been responsible for my injury, and I felt that it had a responsibility to support me. I was angry and disappointed. I wasn't going to leave without a fight. I told him that I had never considered any other career and did not want to be medically retired. The Inspector then began to look at what vacancies there were in non-operational roles. There were some menial administrative roles, which I quickly said that I didn't feel would make best use of my skills. Only at this stage did the Inspector take time to look at my personnel records. He then discovered that I had successfully passed both my Sergeant's and Inspector's promotion examinations and had recently completed a Higher National Diploma in Public Administration. I had also been awarded the School Prize at Initial Training for knowledge of law and procedure.

He finally identified a post for me in the Force Examination Unit, which was responsible for writing and setting examinations for the RUC promotion process. This sounded more like something I could take an interest in and that would make use of my knowledge and skills. It provided a momentary lifting of my gloom and an easing of my anxiety. However, that was to be short-lived, as the Inspector then told me that the reality was that I would never get promoted beyond Inspector. I would not describe myself as promotion-driven, but I had already displayed the abilities to meet the requirements for promotion to Inspector, so suddenly I was being told that this is it, your loss of hearing will prevent your future development. This was the starting point for the first of three new and very different voices which were to direct my future approach to work. This first new voice told me that I needed to work hard, not merely the same as others, but at an optimal level at all times. If I did not, then the consequences would be that I would not succeed, and might lose my job. This voice was part of me; it was in my head, and constantly reminding me to keep working hard.

By the time I went to have my first meeting with the Head of the Examinations Unit I was in a frame of mind that I should be happy to be offered anything. The voice was reminding me that this was a role I could work hard at, and by having this job I would not have to leave the police. As it turned out, I had a natural affinity for the work, and soon settled into my new role. By this stage I had a hearing aid to help with my day-to-day condition. Over the next two years I began to get interested in the area of developing and assessing people. I felt that this work was helping to satisfy the needs of the first voice, and I was feeling more content and positive. I was supported to attend a number of courses. In 1992 I was promoted to Sergeant and began to work on training design and research, as well as continuing the work on writing examinations. I enjoyed the new challenges, and was included in a new team to evaluate police training.

During this successful period of work, over twenty of my colleagues were murdered by terrorists, two of them close friends. This brought about the second new voice in my head, which said that my injury was relatively minor in nature compared to the sacrifices of my colleagues and friends who had lost their lives or who had suffered greater injury, including the loss of limbs or major trauma. This resulted in what is described as "survivor guilt" – a mental condition that occurs when a person perceives that they have done wrong by surviving traumatic events when others did not. This voice was in my head like the first, but it was separate in what it was saying to me. The voice told me that I needed to do everything to the best of my ability and make a difference to those I worked with and the communities I served, as others would never have that opportunity. I now had two separate new voices constantly reminding me of how I needed to behave. These new voices and my response to them focused me and pushed me to the limits of my abilities. I had become a workaholic. This allowed me to succeed in my work, and therefore I could feel better about myself and my guilt and anxiety could lessen.

In 1995 I applied for promotion to Inspector, having received strong support from my supervisors. However, when the application got to my superintendent he reduced the support to conditional, as I could not undertake operational duties. I was not even considered for promotion, and when I asked for feedback, I was informed that the recommendation from my superintendent would mean that no matter how good I was at the job, I would never get an interview for promotion. Once again I was angry, and I felt let down by the organization and took a grievance out against the process. The grievance was investigated by an Assistant Chief Constable. I never did get an official result of the investigation. I was annoyed, and felt envious of those who had been promoted. I recognized that the decision was nothing to do with my ability, but was merely based on the fact that I had a recorded medical condition. The new voices were very loud at this point, especially the first voice, and I put every effort into my work and working long hours. My approach to everything was to avoid mistakes, failure, and disappointment. In parallel to my working life I started to develop myself through academic studies in my own time. In 1998 I successfully completed a Masters in Education and the teaching qualification of a Certificate in Education.

By the next promotion process, the recommendation system had been reviewed and changed. As a result, I was called to interview and was successful in being promoted to Inspector. This brought about the third new voice in my head, that of fighting for fairness and equality. As a result of my experience and my own personal values, I did not want to be accused of not treating people in accordance with their merit and skills. I felt that by pursuing a personal meaningful goal that connected to my values, it would make me feel better about myself.

Unsurprisingly, I worked hard in my new role within the Firearms Department, and found myself involved in a strategic review of the department which required me to write its annual strategy and objectives. This gave me the confidence to apply for a new role as the National Programme Manager on Community and Race Relations, which was required to develop training solutions in the aftermath of the Stephen Lawrence Inquiry Report. The key purpose of this job was to ensure equality, fairness, and diversity were upheld in policing, and this fitted with my third voice. This new role was at the rank of a Temporary Chief Inspector. Success in achieving this role meant that I had broken through the glass ceiling and realized that the barriers that had been previously placed upon me by the Human Resources Inspector could no longer hold me back. This was reinforced by my successful completion of a PhD in Education. A short time later I was successful in being promoted to Chief Inspector. This took place in 2001, at the same time as the transformation from the RUC to the Police Service of Northern Ireland. I was given a new job with responsibility for the training of new student officers at the Police College in Belfast.

My career was on an upward trajectory. In 2006 I successfully applied for a post as superintendent managing the Quality Assurance of the UK National Leadership Academy for Policing. This led in turn to work on International Policing, and subsequently to being a Temporary Chief Superintendent in charge of the International Leadership Unit, and finally the Deputy Head and Strategic Lead of the new National College of Police Leadership in 2010.

It was only in the last couple of years of my service that I was willing to explore the three new voices and perhaps start to come to terms with the circumstances which created them. This is in part due to my own guilt, but also due to there being no system for sharing my feelings with professionals. The response by the RUC to my injury was focused on my physical injury, and little consideration was given to the psychological impact of the injury.

Also, as a police officer there was a heavy emphasis on having to be strong and not showing emotion or weakness.

In the past twenty years I have had the opportunity to be a manager and leader. Each of the four voices has kept me working hard; I probably became a workaholic, always focused on doing my best for the community and being fair and honest with those who work with me or for me. I have developed myself both in terms of academic qualifications and recognized expertise in police education and leadership. I have no doubt that the voices created the drive for me to work harder and over-compensate to prove both to myself and to the organization that I had the necessary skills to be a good police officer and serve the community.

Leadership Reflection

- What stands out for you in this narrative regarding resilience?
- What elements of this narrative link to the aspects of resilience you are working with?
- What other elements of the narrative are important to you, and why?

15

Policing for Peace in Northern Ireland – the Four Voices: Analysis

Every day of the year marks the anniversary of someone's death as a result of the conflict in and about Northern Ireland:

- *3,725 people were killed as a result of the conflict.*
- *Approximately 45,541 people were injured.*
- *There were 36,923 shootings.*
- *16,209 bombings were conducted.*
- *Between 1969 and 1998, 1,533 of the deaths were people under the age of 25; 257 of those killed were under the age of 18.*
- *As of 1998, the largest group (54 per cent) of the deaths and 68 per cent of those injured as a result of the conflict were civilians.*

(Healing Through Remembering (n.d.) Day of Reflection Fact Sheet)

Introduction

In this narrative, Tim shows how resilience is important and has assisted him to succeed through his life and achieve a very high position within the police leadership structure.

The narrative is also inspiring when we look at its bigger picture, and is a symbol of hope for communities all over the world. If we reflect on the changes in Northern Ireland from the 1980s, when Tim joined the Royal Ulster Constabulary, until now, it is a very different Northern Ireland we see. Tim, along with many, many others, has played a part in bringing this about. It is a demonstration of resilience on an individual, organizational, and larger community level, and shows us what can be achieved – good can come from bad; hope from despair; dreams come true; wide-scale benefit can come from resilience.

Voices

Tim identifies four positive voices that he feels are important to him in progressing in his career. Tim highlights that these voices were his own, like a kind of positive self-talk, and the four voices conveyed four different types of messages.

Many people can be quite wary about talking about hearing voices, being concerned they may be suffering from a mental health condition, or that others will think they are. Whilst we do not wish to undermine the difficulties some can experience with negative aspects of hearing voices, we wish to focus here on the positive aspects of self-talk and argue that this is not linked to a mental health condition, and is very common. Tim's narrative demonstrates clearly the positive benefits of these voices.

Do you have voices guiding you in the same way as Tim identifies in the narrative? If so, what are they saying? Is there one consistent message, or as in Tim's case, are several voices saying different things? What are the different voices saying to you? Do you feel the things that are being said are positive or negative? How can these voices assist you in building your resilience?

Contribution

In Tim's narrative, one of the consistent themes we see emerging is his desire to make some form of contribution to the community and society – "doing something to help all society in a particularly difficult time", "doing something positive for the community", "serve the community". This demonstrates a clear sense of larger purpose that is beyond or outside the individual, and as we discussed in Chapter 1, seems to be important in the building of resilience.

Do you think having this sense of larger purpose is important? If you do, what is your purpose, and how do you contribute to your community or wider society? Is this contribution important to you and to others? If so, why, and how do you know?

We also see in this narrative the impact of this sense of larger purpose in terms of resilience, drive, and determination. Tim and his family have clearly experienced some very difficult, hazardous, and frightening situations. During these times, many of Tim's friends and fellow officers were being killed or seriously injured, and many people would simply have walked away from this job and done something else. The example of tenacity, drive, and determination in working towards a larger cause is particularly evident in this case because the financial pressure to continue to just keep working to earn money to live and support family would have been offset to some extent by the compensation and ill health pension he could have received from the RUC if he had been medically discharged from the force. There is clearly something larger for Tim in being a police officer than simply earning money. We also see Tim's resilience in carrying on when he suffers his injury and hearing loss. So why did Tim stay working in the police, do you think? What do you think it is that gives Tim this resilience to continue?

There are no doubt a host of reasons, including upbringing, the need to support his family, finance, and personality, but we argue that a large part of what seems to maintain Tim's tremendous drive and determination is this clear sense of purpose.

Why are you continuing to do what you are doing? How is your resilience helping you to do this?

Injury

Tim's narrative draws out his police force's focus on the physical injuries he sustained in that training incident. We also saw this focus on just the physical in Andrew's narrative in Chapter 6. As Tim identifies, however, and as we discussed in Chapter 7, there are many physical, mental, and spiritual challenges in this type of situation, and all need to be considered, not just the easy to identify and treat physical injuries that are sustained. One of the central arguments in this text is that consideration of your and your employee's makeup in the holistic way identified here is key to building and maintaining resilience – for you, your employees, the organization, and wider society.

Discrimination

In the narrative, we also see the discrimination that Tim experiences because of his disability, and the negative effect this has on him. This type of discrimination is not only experienced by people with hearing loss, of course, and is all too common for people who have many other forms of disability, as well as because of gender, race, sexuality, age, religious belief, and many other reasons. The narrative reveals a little of the negative effects this has on Tim.

It would be rather trite and simplistic to say that Tim's resilience enabled him to overcome the discrimination and its negative effects, and that everyone can do the same. There are obviously many aspects and influences to consider, but Tim's resilience does seem to have played none too small a part in his success and ability to transcend the discrimination he encountered. To challenge, raise grievances, battle, and overcome the obstacles he encountered at a personal level is an inspiration, and at the same time he has been working to bring peace at the larger community level.

It would have been a tremendous loss to many, including the police service and Northern Ireland community, if Tim had given up, walked away, taken medical retirement, or if he had not overcome the discriminatory practices and they had continued, and he had been forced to stay in some "menial administrative role". How many times do leaders, organizations, or society tend to hold people back, limit their potential, or force people into roles that are simply not suitable for that person, and as a result the individual is left unfulfilled and leaders and organizations lose much of what that person can offer?

We invite you to take a moment to reflect. Are you giving all those you lead as much opportunity to grow and shine as you possible can? Can you identify anyone you feel is not in the role that they are best suited to? What about yourself? Does the role you are performing now enable you to realize your full potential?

In the narrative, Tim also identifies one of the other factors that people who are being discriminated against can feel – "I needed to work hard, not merely the same as others, but at an optimal level at all times." Whilst this was no doubt part of the reason for Tim's success, it raises a number of issues. What happens if the person concerned can only do the same as others, and why should they suffer any detrimental effects for doing this? What happens if working at an "optimal level" is not sustainable over the long term? It is easy, then, to anticipate comments from those who are discriminating, such as: "There, I knew the person wasn't capable – couldn't hack it". Tim touches a number of times on the point that he was a workaholic – did the need to work at "optimal level" all the time lead to this? Was being a workaholic linked to his disability? What are the negative consequences on Tim, his family, and the organization of his being a workaholic?

Coleman (1991: 46) argues that people are pushed by regular stress into an addiction to a workaholic lifestyle. He suggests that they get hooked on the adrenaline "kick" they get from working. Woodham (1995: 74) argues that workaholism is an unhelpfully addictive way of coping with stress. Both these points link to our hypervigilance exploration in Chapter 9. Coleman (1991: 46) also points out that whilst workaholics may seem to be great assets, they will only be of short-term benefit to the organization.

Do you or your team experience any of the issues we have discussed above? Is there a possibility you do not know when your employees are experiencing these pressures? What impact do these type of issues have? What can you do about them?

Change

There has been a great deal of change connected to the conflicts that have taken place in Northern Ireland since Tim joined the RUC back in the 1980s. The majority would see these changes that have taken place as very positive.

There are other changes that people in Northern Ireland will have experienced that are not just particular to that location. Aspects such as globalization, staff mobility, changes in demographics, customer and employee expectations, developments in information technology, and the global financial crisis are just some examples. The amount and pace of change seems to be increasing every day, and we argue that this can be one of the main causes of stress, as we identify in Chapter 1, and can cause many people to feel burned out. As a result, a key factor to examine when developing resilience must be how you view change and deal with it. Do you generally see change as bad news that you need to try to resist or avoid, or do you see change as exciting and something to be embraced? What are the implications of these two different views of change? What might be the reasons for your reaction?

Guilt

Tim identifies the survivor guilt he experienced: feeling that he had done something wrong because he survived these traumatic events whilst others did not. These feelings can spark a whole range of questions concerning life, death, good, evil, meaning, and purpose that can be experienced in this type of situation – all examples of the spiritual challenges that can be encountered, and one of the consistent themes that is emerging in this text concerning the development of resilience.

The *Merriam-Webster Dictionary* defines guilt as: "feelings of culpability especially for imagined offenses or from a sense of inadequacy: morbid self-reproach often manifest in marked preoccupation with the moral correctness of one's behaviour".

For employees in general, these feelings of culpability can stem from a whole host of reasons, many related to the organizational context we are primarily considering here: guilt from not being made redundant when many others in the organization have been; guilt from spending too many hours at work and not enough time with family; guilt from being promoted to a leadership position when others in the organization were not; guilt from being involved in an exciting new project when others have to do the more routine but essential maintenance-type activities; and there are many more examples.

We also believe that these feelings of guilt and resulting self-reproach can be cumulative. So we also need to consider the impact if there are feelings of guilt from several sources. This guilt can be difficult to reconcile, and can eat away at your resilience and wear you down.

Do you feel guilty? If so, what for, and why? What effect do these feelings of guilt have on you, and what impact do they have on your resilience?

Death and Dying

The narrative shows that Tim is no stranger to death and having to deal with it, whether in his role as a police officer managing the incidents involved, or as a human being having to come to terms with the death and murder of his friends and colleagues. The box at the beginning of this chapter identifies that 3,725 people were killed as part of the conflict in Northern Ireland, and Tim highlights in his narrative that over twenty of his colleagues and two close friends were murdered. Three hundred police officers were killed during the troubles, and 70 committed suicide.

Tim's narrative is not the only one in this text that shows a person dealing with death. We see it very clearly with Wendy in Chapter 4, and with Eric in

Chapter 10. In Chapter 2, Ginger, in that peak moment in the parking lot, also experiences a time when she is considering the possibility of her own death and is also reconciling the fact that she may well have to take the life of one or two other people. Dealing with death and dying is one of the regular challenges of being a police officer. We said in Chapter 1 that exploring the narratives of police officers would be useful because they are demonstrating huge amounts of resilience as they so often operate at the edges – between life and death, good and evil, right and wrong, health and illness – and we see this time and time again being demonstrated in the narratives in this text.

Some of the officers interviewed in Charles' research describe how one must remain cognizant to maintaining resilience in a world full of human destructiveness and suffering:

> *I've seen officers get sucked into the darkness, I've seen officers commit suicide, and I've seen officers get involved with drugs and alcohol. You play with those things [evil] or you're around those things and if you don't go out and do things that are good, expose yourself to good stuff, and if your life is totally surrounded by negative things; then don't be surprised if you become negative.*
>
> *(Charles 2005: 126)*

One police officer shared his thoughts in this research about the negative or darker side of police work:

> *[There is] day-to-day bombardment of just bad stuff, being around hateful people, and we come after something bad has already happened. So you have this everyday, deal with bad stuff, deal with other people's trash, and somebody's worst 15 minutes of life. It tires you out; it burns you out. Because, I try to give everything I can to that person when in need.*
>
> *(Charles 2005: 126)*

One police officer spoke of evil: "It's overwhelming. You deal with people that are so filled with hate, it's almost like they're possessed. They're so bad and they want to kill you." Another police officer described his beliefs about the evil confronted in police work:

> *We have gotten a good education in what life is really about. There are people out there that do want to kill you and there are people out there that want to kill other people. It's just there's real nastiness in*

our world. I mean Satan is out there and he's active and if people don't
believe that, I think they're fooling themselves.

(Charles 2005: 126)

Of course, seeing and dealing with all this death and destructiveness raises
many questions for the officer in terms of the natural order of things in life:
Why do people die? Why are young innocent children killed? Does this occur
all by chance? Is there a pre-scripted plan? Is there a God directing these events?
All these are spiritual questions which officers are regularly faced with, not
only from themselves, but from the many friends, family, and observers who
are involved and affected by these situations. These experiences are also likely
to cause police officers to reflect upon the ultimate questions about their own
life and death: What will happen to them? How will they die? What about
their loved ones they will leave behind? When so many of the situations that
are experienced involve violent, untimely, painful deaths, is can be difficult to
remain positive.

Many police officers have been immersed in the darker side of society, evil,
and death and destruction. Those identified above in Charles' (2005) research,
and many, many more, first recognize the challenges in front of them. Then
they have each chosen to see themselves through these challenges by looking
at what is most important. The "mission" becomes most important, rather than
the ego, or person.

These police officers learn quickly to focus away from the negativity or
evilness encountered in order to remain resilient:

> *I think my spirituality has helped me learn how to compartmentalize*
> *the bad stuff and put it to the side, focus on the good things, and be able*
> *to leave it at work. I think when you first start, you see so much and*
> *you just hold on to it. If you've got your spirituality, your relationship*
> *with Christ, you can refocus on that when you see bad stuff. (32 year*
> *old female, 14 years in policing).*

(Charles 2005)

Thinking about, reconciling, and coping with our own death is perhaps the
ultimate test of our resilience – previous encounters being a mere prelude to
this ultimate event. Certainly, death is a natural part of life, which we will all
surely have to face sooner or later – unless, of course, you know something we
don't!

One police officer shared his belief about death in police work in Charles' research:

> *Death was the thing that I got my fill of a long time ago. There are obviously different kinds of trauma. But in the "why," there are no answers to those questions that you have. I had to learn that fairly soon. "Why did this little girl die, why did this person die in a traffic wreck?" I just realized that I had to let that go to a higher power because I certainly don't have the answers. (48 year old male, 25 years in policing).*
>
> *(Charles 2005: 123)*

His Holiness the Dalai Lama (in Rinpoche 1992: ix) suggests there are only two ways we can deal with the thought of our own death: we can choose to ignore it, or we can confront the prospect of our own death and, by thinking clearly about it, try to minimize the suffering it can bring. He goes on to argue that most of us would like to die a peaceful death, but suggests we cannot hope to die peacefully if our lives have been full of violence, or if our minds have mostly been agitated by emotions like anger, attachment, or fear. He argues that if we wish to die well, we must learn to live well.

These are powerful points which raise some important questions that we can all reflect upon.

16

Conclusions

As we draw towards the end of this text, we can reflect on the seven powerful narratives from police officers that we have examined in relation to building resilience. These are only a tiny sample of the many amazing stories that countless police officers and leaders more broadly can tell, some of which we have had the privilege to hear as part of our research. We believe everyone has a story to tell about resilience in their lives – what is your story? Why not send it to us, and with your help we can produce another volume, or add it to our Web-based resource at www.policeresilience.com in order to assist others on their journey?

In considering these seven narratives, we have explored a number of themes that stand out in them with respect to developing resilience. We have also raised a number of questions that you may wish to consider and reflect upon. We hope these are of assistance to you. There are many other themes that could be drawn from the narratives, and as we have progressed through the text, we have encouraged you to consider these, discuss them with others, and develop them further. We hope this has been of assistance to you and will continue to be so, and we are keen to hear from you on your explorations and journeys.

There are several consistent messages that come from the narratives, and in closing we would like to say a few words about the things that stand out for us. In line with the rest of this book, we would like to try to convey our message in a slightly different way that we hope will appeal and assist you. We therefore present these conclusions as a written conversation between the two principal authors.

Ginger

So, Jonathan, what do you think have been some of the key messages about resilience that have stood out for you in the narratives?

Jonathan

All too often in the television news, in newspapers and in our general conversations, there is a focus on the negative – the failures and difficulties. What we see in these narratives, however, is a very different picture. Here we see stories of success, of hope, and of inspiration; of people working hard, making enormous sacrifices and contributions to things that are not just about money or bringing benefit for themselves. These people are working towards a larger purpose – building peace, helping vulnerable people, and contributing to communities in crisis. These people are stepping up to the challenge, and there has never been a time when we are so in need of people to step up.

I believe there is a larger purpose to each of our lives.

So one of the themes I see emerging from the narratives, Ginger, is the importance of focusing on and clarifying this larger purpose, this meaning in our own lives, and also taking this to the next stage and thinking through how what we do every day can help in working towards this larger purpose. I think this can help significantly to build and maintain high levels of resilience.

We can perhaps see this most clearly in Tim's narrative in Chapter 14. Although the specific details of what he was doing were constantly changing and he had to be flexible and responsive in what he did, there is no doubt in my mind that Tim has a very clear larger purpose.

Ginger

I would agree, Jonathan, and it also links to personal values, which Sir Peter emphasized in Chapter 12. Certainly, from my perspective, having served as a police officer for over 25 years, I can say this profession has offered me meaning and purpose in my life beyond whatever I could have imagined. As we both have interviewed just under 100 police officers, that theme has shone through continually.

For example, one police commander I recently interviewed shared a story with me. He said he had responded with an officer to assist with an investigation of a domestic disturbance. He described the disturbance as a great amount of yelling and screaming. The woman and man were yelling at each other. The woman's mother was also there, yelling at the other two adults.

The commander was trying hard to gather information from these individuals while also providing cover for the first officer, when a small little girl wandered up to the commander.

He said he would never forget her. He described her as beautiful, dark curls framing her face, and about two or three years old. She had big brown eyes that looked up at him. He said she tapped him on his leg and looked at him and said, "It will be alright," during the middle of this fight between her parents. He said he just about lost it, and began to cry. Here was this little child telling him what an adult should be saying to a child.

He thought about this little girl's words. He recognized that she was also asking him for confirmation that it would be alright. He said he told her yes, it would be okay. What he also knew then was his purpose and meaning. This small child was telling him how important it was for him to be in police work.

This theme of meaning and purpose is not just specific to police work, of course; it is relevant to each one of us in whatever we do. What it relies on is the individual's ability to explore the purpose of his or her own life. Some paths may not reflect the inner peace and strength necessary for the person to find meaning and purpose. Then we must examine whether we are in the right livelihood, or must find a path that resonates with our souls.

Unfortunately, sometimes we are made to work our way through some crises in order to recognize what is of importance, in order to find that meaning and purpose in our lives. I believe this is why police work provides such great examples for all of us.

Jonathan

I am reading your fascinating reflections, Ginger, and writing this response on the train as I rush to yet another meeting. The train is late, I'm feeling frustrated because I will be late for this important meeting, and I am not the only one – the train is packed with angry passengers. As I think about these police officers' narratives and what I learn from them, it reminds me that it is so easy to get caught up, and then lost altogether, in the daily rush, the urgent, and forget about what is important. This draws me back to the prioritizing discussion we had in Chapter 3. It confirms for me that having a clear picture in our minds of our larger purpose and personal values is so important, and one of the key elements in building our resilience to be able to cope with all the stressful events we encounter.

It is hard not to get distracted from this purpose, though, and lose sight of what is important. I think, as we discussed in Chapter 7, in our busy, fast-paced lives with so many things to do and so many demands on our time, we simply have to say "no" more often to things that are not a priority

I am going for an interview this week for a new job. I think it will be a great job, but I am busy at the moment reflecting on my own purpose on Earth and how this new job will enable me to fulfil this purpose, using the values that are important to me. It reminds me again of the quotation from Albert Einstein:

> *You may not think that the world needs you, but it does. For you are*
> *unique, like no one that has ever been before or will come after. No one*
> *can speak with your voice, say your piece, smile your smile, or shine*
> *your light. No one can take your place, for it is yours alone to fill. If you*
> *are not there to shine your light, who knows how many travellers will*
> *lose their way as they try to pass by your empty place in the darkness.*
>
> *(Einstein 1931)*

Ginger

Jonathan, I think this is a constant in all our lives, where we get inundated with past events and ruminations on the future. Our lives become so complex when we move out of the present moment. Certainly, as a police officer, it can become deadly if we are not in the moment of the crisis we are there to resolve, as we saw in Chapter 2.

I believe we can easily get carried away with the emotions involved, become angry, and forget to remain present with everyone in each moment. The stories these officers share show that clearly to me. As they tell their stories, it is apparent that they were there in the story as it happened. I believe it is worrying about past events or wandering into future thoughts that distracts that human being from his or her purpose.

When police officers stray from the path, it is no different than anyone else. They are all just human beings. However, as Sir Peter identified in Chapter 12, we tend to hold police officers to a higher standard – and we should, for they often hold the ultimate decision between life and death. This does, though, put tremendous pressure on officers, and they need high levels of resilience to be able to cope with these high expectations. Again, this is why I think these stories are a tremendous reflection and learning resource for all of us as leaders.

Jonathan

I think we can clearly see this focus on the present in Wendy's narrative in Chapter 4. I have been reflecting on how Wendy managed to get through these terrible experiences. I think it is about remembering your larger purpose, and at the same time staying focused on the present and taking one small step at a time, not thinking too far ahead.

What also stood out from Wendy's narrative was the effort she put into writing her reflective journal. This certainly seemed to assist her to cope and maintain her resilience under very trying circumstances. It was also interesting to note that she describes this as a spiritual practice. Many would label a spiritual practice as prayer or attending church. Whilst these are certainly important practices for many, as Sir Peter identified in Chapter 12, Wendy's practice supports our broad interpretations of both spiritual belief and spiritual practice.

This brings out another aspect that is important, I think, with regard to building resilience. This was drawn out in the analysis of Andrew's narrative in Chapter 7. Sometimes resilience is about letting go, recognizing that there is something much bigger than us, and that we cannot control or manage everything. We just have to let go and trust in what is bigger than any of us.

Ginger

One of the interesting things that I noted in the stories was how clear each officer was with the experience they shared. It was truly fascinating to read how focused each police officer was as they wrote their story. This was so consistent throughout each case.

When I have interviewed other police officers, I have found they have given just a little thought to the question asked of them, and then within minutes the officer has been able to recall an event with such clarity and detail that I felt as if I was there with them at the moment described. This always brings to the front of my mind how significant and powerful our stories are, the importance of telling the stories with all of our being, and the capability to listen to ourselves and each other as we tell our stories.

I believe that we must keep telling the stories. Certainly, the importance of storytelling is paramount to certain cultures in our society, whilst many other cultures seem to have lost this important aspect to life. It allows the listener and the storyteller a moment in time to share their hearts and minds.

For leaders, understanding the importance of telling stories provides a moment with another individual, showing respect for each other by paying attention. As Sir Peter highlighted in Chapter 12, "give them the space to talk to you". We show this respect by *listening* to others and finding value in each others' experiences. We lead by sharing our stories with others and with our employees, with the intent of demonstrating valuable lessons and examples. It can also indicate, in very powerful ways that are easy to see, our history, our values, and our beliefs, what we hold dear and think is important, and the effective ways to act.

Jonathan

And it never ceases to amaze me, you know, how many really powerful and humbling stories police officers have to tell. You all experience so much. I have so much respect for you all and what you do, and I feel an enormous debt of gratitude to you all for doing your best to keep me, my family, friends, community, and society safe. I want to help you as much I am able in whatever way is useful. I also think I and others can learn a great deal from you all.

One aspect of Ron's and Eric's stories, in Chapters 8 and 10, stood out for me, and links to the commander's experience with the little girl you told us about earlier, and which returns to something I touched on with regard to small moments and to Wendy's narrative in Chapter 4. This is, interestingly, at the other end of the scale to my point earlier regarding finding clarity of meaning and purpose in your life. Ron and Eric show us also that it is often the smallest, briefest, and seemingly insignificant moments that can have the biggest impact, and can lift us and stay with us forever, continually there boosting our resilience.

Another factor I think that helps to maintain our resilience is keeping a positive mindset. This links to the positive and negative spirals we explored in

Chapter 9. It can be difficult sometimes not to be swinging down the negative spiral, but I wonder whether it is just about clocking in our minds which spiral we are on and remembering to keep focused on the positive. This may be assisted by the positive self-talk and listening to our own voices that Sir Peter identified in Chapter 12, and that Tim identified in Chapter 14 as such a powerful influence in his life.

As well as the things that stood out for you in the narratives, Ginger, I was just thinking then about what key aspects about building resilience you would like us to encourage the reader to reflect upon, and do you think that these have come out in the narratives?

Ginger

Very good thought here, Jonathan. Perhaps the most compelling feature is one of *respect*. I believe respect, civility, and compassion, as illustrated in each story, brings the officer, those involved in the story, and the readers into the environment of resilience using respect, civility, and compassion. Here again, we see police officers willing to share deep thoughts and beliefs with anyone willing to listen. They share these touching, minute moments that demonstrate huge learning for them and the reader, sometimes years later, in the hope that they can assist the reader too.

Perhaps we can get too wrapped up in thinking and making all of this is too difficult with respect to developing resilience, and we can start to think we will never get there. The stories illustrate for me the importance of remembering that it can be simple, as simple as centring oneself and remembering what is most important to find our meaning and purpose, and then sharing that with the world. That concept can heal us in our souls and heal those we come in contact with in this world. Can it be that simple? I think these police officers tell us it can, whether they recognize it or not.

Jonathan

I think you are right, Ginger; I can certainly overcomplicate things sometimes. It is always useful to keep it as simple as we can. I like the KISS acronym: "Keep It Simple, Stupid."

Keeping it simple reminds me of Andrew's narrative in Chapter 6, where he emphasized how a time of just being, enforced on him by his injury, and moving away from the business of doing was so beneficial for him in coping with his difficult experience. The message for me here is that in developing resilience, it is useful sometimes just to be, just to take time to relax and be with yourself, your family, and your friends.

Ginger

Jonathan, one of the questions I was considering with regard to these police officers' narratives was where the front line was for each of them. Each story seems to demonstrate the officers' ability to work, live, and function in their respective communities. In Chapter 2, the officer is continuing to live in the same neighbourhood where this critical incident occurred.

In Wendy's chapter, she is working in a disaster area. There is shooting and rioting all around her. Yet she is resilient in her feelings about how important her work is to the community; it appears to be a recognition of the larger whole rather than the individual. In Andrew's chapter, his belief about the work and its importance seems to propel him through the darkness of his injury.

Eric's chapter demonstrates how one relationship with a homeless man changed his life and beliefs as a cop. He and his friend make a connection and share time together, each recognizing the other's shortcomings, whether it be Eric's short tenure as a police officer or the homeless man's addictions. They become friends. Again, it appears to be a disintegration of the individual's personal barrier or front line, and an integration into community.

Ron's chapter illustrates his acceptance of his mistakes and recognition of growth and the community's willingness to accept Ron as he learns the job. It is his learning that gives him strength and resilience through the difficult periods where there appears to be no hope or when discouragement reigns. Perhaps, as leaders, we can find our resilience by actually living and loving in the communities where we work and reside. Instead of hiding in the house and running from the garage to the car to get to work, we can immerse ourselves and find the richness in our communities in similar ways to the ways these police officers have shared with us.

Jonathan

Fascinating reflections, Ginger. You have such a wonderful way with words that really brings out some useful new insights and causes me to reflect. This issue about connection is regularly identified, and seems to be an important aspect to the spiritual dimension. It reminds me of the British poet Alfred Lord Tennyson's description of his experience of this connection:

> *All at once, as it were out of the intensity of the consciousness of individuality, the individuality itself seemed to dissolve and fade away into boundless being, and this is not a confused state, but the clearest of the clearest, the surest of the surest … utterly beyond words.*
>
> *(Tennyson n.d.: 4)*

It is very interesting to think that a focus on others rather than ourselves can not only be of tremendous benefit to others, the community and wider society, but can also reap enormous rewards for us in terms of building our own resilience.

I think your call to all of us to get more involved in our communities is very powerful, and may be a great point on which to draw our discussion here to a close. There are so many points we could discuss about the narratives that have been shared with us, so many more ideas, thoughts, and theories we could bring in, but sometimes less is more, and the narratives are so powerful I think they speak so much for themselves.

I am not quite sure how to finish this book, or this final chapter, so I will hand over to you, Ginger, to end with more of those wonderful words of yours that dance on the page.

Ginger

How can I finish something that is not yet finished?! Let's think about what we have acquired here in these printed pages. We have our stories. They make us rich in character. They provide opportunity for change, growth, love, and peace, and the book offers you choices to make. One choice is that you can embrace the opportunity you have in front of you. The other choice is to ignore the stories, plod along without purpose, or focus on something "shiny", quick or superficial.

The danger if we choose the latter is that we can fall out of sync with ourselves and who we really are deep inside. We are all wonderful, and even with all our frailties and flaws, we have so much potential, so much to offer each other if we are willing to take the time. Certainly, these police officers have offered us significant moments in their lives to add to our learning. It is the gift of caring.

As you are reading this book, please do not imagine that police officers are superheroes, and as a result think you could not possibly do similar things. They are only ordinary human beings, even though they are doing some extraordinary things using extraordinary skills. Many police officers do, of course, fall off the path, sometimes repeatedly. They can become cynical and broken. They can become bitter and angry, and experience horrendous health issues. What this exploration about resilience shows us, though, is that we can all fall, but if we build our resilience, this can bring us to the point where we can stand again – similar to that superhero who manages to re-create himself from his one character flaw.

All we have is time together. We have time to share and learn and teach each other. We hope these stories have brought some peace and love as well as resilience to your life. We hope you share your story. There are those around you waiting to hear it.

References

ACPO (Association of Chief Police Officers) (2011) *Statement of Mission and Values for the Police Service*. Available at http://acpoprofessionalethics.org/default.aspx?page=somav (accessed 25 October 2012).

ACPO (2012) *The National Decision Model*. Available at http://www.acpo.police.uk/documents/president/201201PBANDM.pdf (accessed 11 April 2013).

Adair, J. and Nelson, J. (ed.) (2004) *Creative Church Leadership*. Norwich: Canterbury Press.

Alexander, D.A., Klein, S., Falconer, M. and Woolnough, P. (2012) "Resilience and Well-being in a Scottish Police Force". In *Scottish Institute for Policing Research Annual Report 2011*. Available at http://www.sipr.ac.uk/downloads/SIPR_Annual_Report_11.pdf (accessed 25 October 2012).

Altman, Y. (2010) "In Search of Spiritual Leadership: Making a Connection with Transcendence". *Human Resource Management International Digest*, vol. 18, no. 6.

APA (American Psychological Association) (2012) *Marriage and Divorce* http://www.apa.org/topics/divorce/index.aspx (accessed 25 October 2012).

Bakan, J. (2005) *The Corporation: The Pathological Pursuit of Profit and Power*. New York: Free Press.

Barrett, R. (2003) "Culture and Consciousness. Measuring Spirituality in the Workplace by Mapping Values". In Giacalone, R.A. and Jurkiewicz, C. (ed.) *Handbook of Workplace Spirituality and Organizational Performance*. New York: M.E. Sharpe.

Barrett, R. (2006) *Building a Values-driven Organisation: A Whole System Approach to Cultural Transformation*, Boston, MA: Butterworth-Heinemann.

Bayliss, V., Ciarrochi, J. and Deane, F.P. (2010) "On Being Mindful, Emotionally Aware and More Resilient: A Longitudinal Pilot Study of Police Recruits". *Australian Psychologist* (December), vol. 45, no. 4, pp. 274–82.

Beddoes-Jones F. (2012) "Authentic Leadership: The Key to Building Trust". *People Management* (August).

Begley, S. (2007) *Train Your Mind, Change Your Brain: How a New Science Reveals Our Extraordinary Potential to Transform Ourselves*. New York: Random House.

Bennet, T. (1994) "Recent Developments in Community Policing". In Stephens, M. and Becker, S. (ed.) *Police Force, Police Service: Care and Control in Britain*. London: Macmillan.

Bloom, S (1997) *Creating Sanctuary: Toward an Evolution of Sane Societies*, New York: Routledge.

Bouckaert, L. and Zsolnai, L. (ed.) (2011) *The Palgrave Handbook of Spirituality and Business*. Basingstoke: Palgrave Macmillan.

Burbeck, E. and Furnham, A. (1985) "Police Officer Selection: A Critical Review of the Literature". *Journal of Police Science and Administration*, no. 13, pp. 58–69.

Business in the Community (2008) *Emotional Resilience Toolkit*. Available at http://www.bitc.org.uk/resources/publications/emotional_resilience.html (accessed 25 October 2012).

Carlier, I.V.E. (1999) "Finding Meaning in Police Traumas". In Violanti, J.M. and Paton, D.J. (ed.) *Police Trauma: Psychological Aftermath of Civilian Combat*. Springfield, IL: Charles C. Thomas, pp. 227–33.

Casey, Judi and Corday, Karen (2007) "Conversations with the Experts: Personal and Workplace Resilience. An Interview with Kay N. Campbell". *Network News*, vol. 9, no. 3. Available at http://workfamily.sas.upenn.edu/sites/workfamily.sas.upenn.edu/files/imported/archive/networknews/The_Network_News_Interview_33.pdf (accessed 11 April 2013).

Chang, K. (2008) "Edward N. Lorenz, a Meteorologist and a Father of Chaos Theory, Dies at 90". *New York Times*, 17 April. Available at http://www.nytimes.com/2008/04/17/us/17lorenz.html?_r=0 (accessed 11 April 2013).

Charles, G.L. (2005) *How Spirituality is Incorporated in Police Work: A Qualitative Study*. UMI Dissertation Services, UMI no. 3181920. Ann Arbor, MI: Proquest.

Charles, G.L. (2009) "How Spirituality is Incorporated in Law Enforcement". *FBI Law Enforcement Bulletin*, vol. 78, no. 5.

Chopra, D. (2010) *Research on Happiness Quotient*. Lakewood, CO: Mile Hi Church.

CIPD (Chartered Institute of Personnel and Development) (2010) *Employee Outlook Survey July*. London: CIPD.

CIPD (2011a) *CIPD/Simplyhealth Absence Management Survey*. London: CIPD.

CIPD (2011b) *Developing Resilience: An Evidence-based Guide for Practitioners*. London: CIPD.

Coleman, V. (1991) *Stress Management Techniques*. London: Gold Arrow Publications.

Cornum, R. (2012) "Can we Teach Resilience? Brigadier General Rhonda Cornum on Emotional Fitness". Presentation at the Young Foundation, London, 7 February. Available at http://www.youngfoundation.org/general-/-all/events/

can-we-teach-resilience-brigadier-general-rhonda-cornum-emotional-fitness (accessed 25 October 2012).

Covey, S.R. (1989) *7 Habits of Highly Effective People*. London: Simon and Schuster.

Covey, S.R. (1999) *Principle-centred Leadership*. London: Simon and Schuster.

Czander, W.M. (1993) *The Psychodynamics of Work and Organizations*. London: Guilford Press.

Einstein, A. (1931) *Living Philosophies*. New York: Simon and Schuster.

Esmond, J. (2012) *Stress Levels are Rising Worldwide*. Available at http://www. gostress.com/stress-levels-are-rising-worldwide/ (accessed 25 October 2012).

Fielding, N.G. and Conroy, S. (1994) "Against the Grain: Co-operation in Child Sexual Abuse Investigations". In Stephens, M. and Becker, S. (ed.) *Police Force, Police Service: Care and Control in Britain*. London: Macmillan.

Figley, C. (1999) "Police Compassion Fatigue (PCF): Theory, Research, Assessment, Treatment, and Prevention". In Violanti, J.M. and Paton, D.J. (ed.) *Police Trauma: Psychological Aftermath of Civilian Combat*. Springfield, IL: Charles C. Thomas, pp. 37–53.

Fontana, D. (2003) *Psychology, Religion, and Spirituality*. Malden, MA: Blackwell.

Frankl, V. (1984) *Man's Search for Meaning*. New York: Washington Square Press.

Fry, L.W. (2003) "Toward a Theory of Spiritual Leadership". *The Leadership Quarterly*, no. 14, pp. 693–727.

Freedman, J. (2002) *Hijacking of the Amygdala*. Available at: http://www.myevt. com/news/retrain-your-brain-learn-amygdala-hijack (accessed 11 April 2013).

Fry, L.W. (2005) "Toward a Theory of Ethical and Spiritual Wellbeing and Corporate Social Responsibility through Spiritual Leadership". In Giacalone, C., Jurkiewicz, C. and Dunn, C., *Positive Psychology in Business Ethics and Corporate Responsibility*. Greenwich, CT: Information Age, pp. 47–83.

Gilmartin, K.M. (2002) *Emotional Survival for Law Enforcement: A Guide for Officers and Their Families*. Tucson, AZ: E-S Press.

Goffman, E. (1987) *The Presentation of Self in Everyday Life*. Harmondsworth: Penguin.

Goleman, D. (2005) *Emotional Intelligence*. London: Bloomsbury.

Green, A. and Humphrey, J. (2012) *Coaching for Resilience: A Practical Guide to Using Positive Psychology*. London: Kogan Page.

Gregory, J. (1996) *The Psychosocial Education of Nurses: The Interpersonal Dimension*. Aldershot: Avebury.

Guirdham, M. (1995) *Interpersonal Skills at Work*. London: Prentice-Hall.

Harung, H., Travis, F., Pensgaard, A., Boes, R., Cook-Greuter, S. and Daley, K. (2009) "Higher Psycho-physiological Refinement in World-class Norwegian Athletes: Brain Measures of Performance Capacity". *Scandinavian Journal of Medicine and Science in Sports*, pp. 1–10.

Healing Through Remembering (n.d.) *Day of Reflection Fact Sheet*. Available at http://www.dayofreflection.com/pdf/fact_sheet_on_the_conflict_in_and_about_northern_ireland_2.pdf (accessed 25 October 2012).

Herrick, Jack et al. (2011) *How to Eat Properly*. Available at http://www.wikihow.com/Eat-Properly (accessed 25 October 2012).

Hills, J. (2012) "Fit Staff are Productive Staff". *People Management* (October).

Holdaway, S. (1989) "Discovering Structure: Studies of the British Police Occupational Culture". In Weatheritt, M. (ed.) *Police Research: Some Future Prospects*. Aldershot: Avebury.

Holdaway, S. (1994) "Recruitment, Race and the Police Subculture". In Stephens, M. and Becker, S. (ed.) *Police Force, Police Service: Care and Control in Britain*. London: Macmillan.

Howard, S. (2010) "Spirituality and the Holistic Development Model: Influences on Personal Leadership". Presentation at the British Association for the Study of Spirituality *Spirituality in a Changing World* Conference, 4–6 May, Windsor, UK.

Howard, S. and Smith, J.A. (2011) "Interview with Chief Constable Adrian Lee". *International Journal of Leadership in Public Services*, 2nd special issue, *Values, Spirituality and Leadership (Part 2)*, guest editors Gilbert, P. and Fulford, K.W.M., vol. 7, no. 2, pp. 131–7.

HSE (Health and Safety Executive) (2010) *Work Related Stress*. Available at http://www.hse.gov.uk/stress/ (accessed 25 October 2012).

Hufton, D.R. (2013) *Spirit of the Act: Exploring Constructs Underpinning Police Officers' Decisions*. Unpublished PhD thesis, Leeds Metropolitan University.

Kirschman, E. (2006) *I Love a Cop: What Police Families Need to Know*. New York: Guilford Press.

Kolb, D.A. (1983) *Experiential Learning: Experience as the Source of Learning and Development*. London: Prentice-Hall.

Kriger, M. and Seng, Y. (2005) "Leadership with Inner Meaning: A Contingency Theory of Leadership based on the Worldviews of Five Religions". *The Leadership Quarterly*, no. 16, pp. 771–806.

Lazarus, R.S. (1966) *Psychological Stress and the Coping Process*. New York: McGraw-Hill.

Lips-Wiersma, M. and Morris, L. (2011a) *The Map of Meaning: A Guide to Sustaining Our Humanity in the World of Work*. Sheffield: Greenleaf Publishing.

Lips-Wiersma, M. and Morris, L. (2011b) "Voicing Meaningfulness at Work". In Bouckaert, L. and Zsolnai, L. (ed.) *The Palgrave Handbook of Spirituality and Business*. Basingstoke: Palgrave Macmillan.

Loehr, J. and Schwartz, T. (2003) *The Power of Full Engagement: Managing Energy, Not Time, is the Key to High Performance and Personal Renewal*. New York: Free Press.

Malcolm, A.A. (2010) "Spirituality, Religion and Work: A Study of the Impact of Faith on Police Employees". Unpublished MRes. dissertation, Manchester Metropolitan University.

Maslow, A.H. (1968) *Towards a Psychology of Being*. New York: D. Von Nostrand.

Maslow, A.H. (1994) *Religions, Values, and Peak Experiences*. Harmondsworth: Penguin Arkana.

Mauboussin, M.J. (2012) "The True Measures of Success". *Harvard Business Review* (October).

Millet, B. (2012) "Half of All CEOs Feel Isolated and Lonely at the Top". Available at http://www.ceotoceo.com/half-of-all-ceos-feel-isolated-and-lonely-at-the-top/ (accessed 25 October 2012).

Moustakas, C. (1994) *Phenomenological Research Methods*. London: Sage.

Nixon, P. (1976) "The Human Function Curve. With special reference to Cardiovascular Disorders: Part II", *Practitioner*, vol. 217, (December), pp. 935–44.

Nixon, P.G. (1982) "Stress and the Cardiovascular System". *Practitioner*, vol. 226, no. 1,371, pp. 1,589–98.

Perez, D.W. and Shtull, P.R. (2002) "Police Research and Practice: An American Perspective". *Police Practice and Research*, vol. 3, no. 3.

Personnel Today (2001) "Workplace Stress Takes its Toll". *Personnel Today* (1 December). Available at http://www.personneltoday.com/Articles/08/03/2002/11462/Workplace-stress-takes-its-toll.htm (accessed 25 October 2012).

Peterson, Suzanne J., Balthazard, Pierre A., Waldman, David A. and Thatcher, Robert W. (2008) "Neuroscientific Implications of Psychological Capital: Are the Brains of Optimistic, Hopeful, Confident, and Resilient Leaders Different?". *Organisational Dynamics*, vol. 37, no. 4, pp. 342–53.

Rayment, J.J. and Smith, J.A. (2011) *MisLeadership: Prevalence, Causes and Consequences*. Farnham: Gower.

Rayment, J.J. and Smith, J.A. (2013) "The Current and Future Role of Business Schools". *The Journal of Finance and Management in Public Services*. vol. 11, no. 2, pp. 478–94.

Rees, B. and Smith, J.A. (2008) "Breaking the Silence: The Traumatic Circle of Policing". *International Journal of Police Science and Management*, vol. 7, no. 2, pp. 137–54.

Rinpoche, S. (1992) *The Tibetan Book of Living and Dying*. London: Random House.

River Path Associates (2002) *This Brave and Resolute Stand: Serving in the Royal Ulster Constabulary*, Belfast: RUC George Cross Foundation. Northern Ireland. Available at http://www.rucgcfoundation.org/pdf/brave.pdf (accessed 11 April 2013).

Roberts, C. (2012) *Checklist for Personal Values.* Available at http://www. selfcounseling.com/help/personalsuccess/personalvalues.html (accessed 25 October 2012).

Rokeach, M. (1979) *Understanding Human Values: Individual and Societal.* New York. Free Press.

Rothberg, D. (1993) "The Crises of Modernity and the Emergence of Socially Engaged Spirituality". *ReVision*, vol. 17, no. 3, pp. 105–14.

Schön, D.A. (1983) *The Reflective Practitioner: How Professionals Think in Action.* New York: Basic Books.

Schwartz, S.H. (2006) *Basic Human Values: An Overview.* Jerusalem: The Hebrew University of Jerusalem. Available at http://segr-did2.fmag.unict.it/Allegati/convegno%207-8-10-05/Schwartzpaper.pdf (accessed 11 April 2013).

Scott, E. (2011) *Cope With Stress and Become More Resilient.* Available at http://stress. about.com/od/positiveattitude/ht/resilient.htm (accessed 25 October 2012).

Seyle, H. (1956) *The Nature of Stress.* Available at http://www.icnr.com/articles/the-nature-of-stress.html (accessed 25 October 2012).

Smith, J.A. (2005) *Training for the Whole Person: An Exploration of Possibilities for Enhancing the Spiritual Dimension of Police Training.* PhD dissertation, University of Hull.

Smith, J.A. and Charles, G. (2010) "The Relevance of Spirituality in Policing: A Dual Analysis". *International Journal of Police Science and Management*, vol. 12, no. 3, pp. 320–38.

Smith, J.A. and Charles, G. (forthcoming) *Spirituality as a Strategy for Coping with the Challenges of Police Work.*

Smith, J.A. and Malcolm, A.A. (2010) "Spirituality, Leadership and Values in the NHS". *International Journal of Leadership in Public Services*, vol. 6, no. 2, pp. 39–53.

Smith, J.A. and Rayment, J.J. (2007) "The Global SMP Fitness Framework: A Guide for Leaders Considering the Relevance of Spirituality in the Workplace". *Management Decision Journal*, vol. 45, no. 2, pp. 217–34.

Stephens, M. and Becker, S. (ed.) (1994) *Police Force, Police Service: Care and Control in Britain.* London: Macmillan.

Sutton, R. (2009) "How to Be a Good Boss in a Bad Economy". *Harvard Business Review*, vol. 87, no. 6, pp. 42–50.

Tennant, M. (1993) *Psychology and Adult Learning.* London: Routledge.

Tennyson, H. (n.d.) "Alfred Lord Tennyson: A Memoir by His Son". In Harung, H., Heaton, D., Graff, W. and Alexander, C. (1996) "Peak Performance and Higher States of Consciousness: A Study of World-class Performers". *Journal of Managerial Psychology*, vol. 11, no. 4, p. 4.

Travis, F. (2009) "Brain Functioning as the Ground for Spiritual Experiences and Ethical Behavior". *FBI Law Enforcement Bulletin*, vol. 78, no. 5.

Travis, F., Tecce, J., Arenander, A. and Wallace, R. (2002) "Patterns of EEG Coherence, Power, and Contingent Negative Variation Characterize the Integration of Transcendental and Waking States". *Biological Psychology*, vol. 61, no. 3, pp. 293–319.

Trungpa, C. (2009) *Smile at Fear: Awakening the True Heart of Bravery*. Boston, MA: Shambhala Publications.

Violanti, J.M. and Paton, D.J. (1999) *Police Trauma: Psychological Aftermath of Civilian Combat*. Springfield, IL: Charles C. Thomas.

Walker, N. (1994) "Care and Control in the Police Organisation". In Stephens, M. and Becker, S. (ed.) *Police Force, Police Service: Care and Control in Britain*. London: Macmillan.

Walsh, R.J. (2008) Presentation at the FBI Police Academy's *Spirituality: The DNA of Law Enforcement* Conference, Leesburg, VA, 15–23 June.

Wilber, K. (2001) *The Eye of Spirit: An Integral Vision for a World Gone Slightly Mad*. London: Shambhala Publications.

Wilson, S. and Ferch, S. (2005) "Enhancing Resilience in the Workplace Through the Practice of Caring Relationships". *Organisation Development Journal*, vol. 23, no. 4, pp. 45–60.

Woodham, A. (1995) *Beating Stress at Work*. London: Health Education Authority.

Zohar, D. and Drake, J. (2000) "On the Whole". *People Management*, vol. 6, no. 8, p. 55.

Index

If you have found this book useful you may be interested in other titles from Gower

Collaborative Wisdom
From Pervasive Logic to Effective
Operational Leadership
Greg Park
Hardback: 978-1-4094-3460-3
Ebook – PDF: 978-1-4094-3461-0
Ebook – ePUB: 978-1-4094-7354-1

Managing Responsibly
Alternative Approaches to Corporate
Management and Governance
Edited by Jane Buckingham and Venkataraman Nilakant
Hardback: 978-1-4094-2745-2
Ebook – PDF: 978-1-4094-2746-9
Ebook – ePUB: 978-1-4094-6044-2

Third Generation Leadership and the Locus of Control
Knowledge, Change and Neuroscience
Douglas G. Long
Hardback: 978-1-4094-4453-4
Ebook – PDF: 978-1-4094-4454-1
Ebook – ePUB: 978-1-4094-8329-8

GOWER

Delivering High Performance
The Third Generation Organisation
Douglas G. Long
Hardback: 978-1-4724-1332-1
Ebook – PDF: 978-1-4724-1333-8
Ebook – ePUB: 978-1-4724-1334-5

Effective Multi-Unit Leadership
Local Leadership in Multi-Site Situations
Chris Edger
Hardback: 978-1-4094-2432-1
Ebook – PDF: 978-1-4094-2433-8
Ebook – ePUB: 978-1-4094-6041-1

Choosing Leaders and Choosing to Lead
Science, Politics and Intuition in Executive Selection
Douglas Board
Hardback: 978-1-4094-3648-5
Ebook – PDF: 978-1-4094-3649-2
Ebook – ePUB: 978-1-4094-8701-2

Visit **www.gowerpublishing.com** and

- search the entire catalogue of Gower books in print
- order titles online at 10% discount
- take advantage of special offers
- sign up for our monthly e-mail update service
- download free sample chapters from all recent titles
- download or order our catalogue